I0054328

SELLING
THE
TRUTH

A "SEMOIR" WITH INSIGHTS
FOR LIFE AND BUSINESS

by

HERSH REPHUN

Copyright 2024 by Hersh Rephun.
SELLING THE TRUTH: A "Semoir" with Insights for Life and Business.
All Rights Reserved

Published by Leadership Books,
Inc. Las Vegas, Nevada – New York,
New York
LeadershipBooks.com

ISBN:
978-1-965401-36-1 (Hardcover)
978-1-965401-37-8 (Paperback)
978-1-965401-38-5 (eBook)

All Rights Reserved. No part of this publication may be reproduced, distributed, or transmitted in any form or by any means, including photocopying, recording, or other electronic or mechanical methods, without the prior written permission of the publisher, except in the case of brief quotations embodied in critical reviews and certain other noncommercial uses permit-ted by copyright law.

Leadership Books, Inc is committed to publishing works of quality and integrity. In that spirit, we are proud to offer this book to our readers; however, the story, the experiences, and the words are the authors alone. The conversations in the book all come from the author's recollections, not word-for-word transcripts. All of the events are true to the best of the author's memory. The author, in no way, represents any company, corporation, or brand mentioned herein. The views expressed are solely those of the author.

ACKNOWLEDGMENTS

When you write your first book at 57 years old, there are a lot of people to thank. Every client I have ever worked with deserves my thanks; championing your brands has been an honor and a joy. Appreciation also goes to Mrs. Nestler, my second-grade teacher, who cast me as the "Scarecrow" in our grade-school production of "The Wizard of Oz," and Dr. Anthony S. Beukas of YU/YCDS, who cast me as "Mozart" in our college production of "Amadeus."

I want to thank my wife, Devon, who has supported me in all that you're about to read, and when you do, you'll have a sense of the debt I owe her; my children, Menachem, Aryeh, Tessa, Keaton, and Samantha—you are the only *why* I have or need; my sisters, Donna and Hilary, my family and friends—oh, what you've been through, raising a baby into a man when he had no idea who he was or should be—that was no mean feat. My mom and dad, Josh and Claire Rephun, set an astonishingly high bar for honesty and integrity, while creating a home filled with love, warmth, and laughter. Both gone way too soon and missed beyond expression. My thanks to them is reserved for last because whatever gifts or goodness I possess were bestowed on me by them the day I was born.

FOREWORD

Here's what I love about Hersh and his first "semoir" so aptly titled *Selling the Truth.* Everything.

We've worked together for almost two decades (as his friend and client), in pursuits spanning publicity, comedy, podcasting, events, and just having a barrel of laughs over modestly priced sushi. Hersh lives life to the fullest, and there's one consistent trait that shines through all he does: He commits. He commits to his clients, to his family and friendships, to philosophies and tactics. He's someone to emulate, and *Selling the Truth* is your practical guidebook for living as your committed, authentic self.

The first time I saw Hersh do standup comedy, the show was upstairs at a bar in Hollywood. After a few unmemorable joke-slingers did sets, Hersh took the stage in the character of a German performer whose star has somewhat faded. Not your ordinary comedy act, and one that required the audience to change gears and buy into a "far out" premise. After the crowd's initial "what the f is going on?" reaction, he quickly won them over and crushed it! For twenty minutes, he stayed in character and improvised ninety percent of his act in that accent. That is commitment. He knew what was funny to him and did what he wanted to do. He trusted himself. (By the way, if Hersh is reading this book for the audio version, please sir, I beg you to read this foreword in that thick German accent.)

Selling the Truth navigates the landscape of personal and professional branding with a quirky blend of memoir and Hersh's practical, albeit sage advice. Each chapter dives deeper into the need for authenticity and stresses the importance of integrity. Knowing oneself is half the battle to crafting one's "brand identity", and now, we have a template to discover our own truths.

Hersh challenges us to embrace truth as our greatest asset in the journey of self-discovery. This guy is a living breathing "legacy brand", and we should all thank him for sharing his self-discoveries.

— Jordan Brady, filmmaker and founder,
Commercial Directing Film School

CONTENTS

Dedication

For Tehila: *Be true to yourself, love your incredible parents, and keep laughing!*

TRUTH TASTES FUNNY

Humans. Hysterical, right?

All these complex systems that make our bodies run, pumping blood to our brains where the most ridiculous thoughts swirl so feverishly that we become like one of those wind-up helicopter toys found in breakfast cereal, our emotional rubber bands holding incredible tension and ready to spin out at any moment. One could argue that we are so confounded by our frayed tether to reality that we've engineered a tool called "Artificial Intelligence" (AI) to get us off the hook. So terrified are we of our own minds that we've willingly replaced them with apps, social media, and virtual reality. And then, we have the audacity to be deathly afraid that AI will replace us (after all, AI was one of the biggest stories of 2023, and for all its utility and misuse, the notion that it controls us may be the funniest-tasting truth of all)! Or maybe...

Maybe the funniest-tasting truth is how difficult we sometimes find it to fathom our own ridiculousness. If our biology exists

(Matrix-like theories aside), why is it hard to believe that we are addicted to pratfalls? To live on Earth is to engage in a continuous cover-up of our vulnerability. This façade of fortitude infects our otherwise beautiful beings with Jolly Green Giant Disease, or Goliath Syndrome (whichever one won't result in a cease-and-desist order), whereby we must puff ourselves up and set impossible goals for ourselves that we pretend to accomplish (or that we achieve at the price of our humanity).

I know, this is kinda heavy. You heard I was funny. And I am. Believe me, if you'd seen me at five years old mimicking Rich Little's impersonation of Richard Nixon (fingers wagging along with "I am not a crook!") while shaking my naked butt in front of my sisters, it would remove any doubt. But whether it's a refusal to acknowledge climate change when our only hope in fighting wildfires is the emergence of a sudden typhoon, or something as personal as our own ideas about what career we should pursue or what life we should lead, we would rather change the mirror than work on our reflection.

It seems we have a problem, to be sure, but we can't solve a problem without establishing its presence. In this case, fear of the truth is the problem. And to go along with that fear, we appear to be confused about "truth" as a concept. We profess to live in a "post-truth world," but without the anchor of truth, nothing can be verified. We have no idea what the h*ll we are doing here (or why placing asterisks in place of certain letters creates a softer impression than using those letters, or whether it's acceptable to substitute other characters to get our d#$% point across!).

The good news is, we are *not* living in an age of unverifiable truth, nor are we doomed to failure as a species (note that I said "failure," not "extinction"—there's nothing we can do about extinction but at least we can die a *success*!). Yes, we live in an environment where facts vary, depending on where you get your truth. That's a tough one. But rather than try to impose absolute verifiable reality on one another, why not take off the blinders (as my seventh-grade social studies teacher, Mrs. Strachman, used to urge us), step outside ourselves, gain some perspective, and see what our own private reality has to offer?

To what end, you ask? This "truth" stuff seems awfully ethereal. Is there a practical purpose here? I hate to reward your impatience, but yes, the other side of the equation is the first word of the book title: *selling*. Selling the Truth. Veracity on purpose. Building our brands and businesses from the inside out in pursuit of success in whatever ways we define it. That's what this book is about.

THE BIG IDEA HERE IS THAT WE MUST STOP BEING AFRAID OF REALITY AND SEEK TO EMBRACE TRUTH AS OUR ALLY, AS OUR WEAPON OF CHOICE IN THE GAME OF LIFE, BUSINESS, AND BRAND-BUILDING.

Although I have spent the last 30 years showing others how to brand their products, services, and even themselves, I've harbored a resistance to overt "*selling*." Selling for me has meant putting my wants and hunger ahead of the needs of others. I've equated selling with pushing, a manipulation in which you end up with something you didn't want, and I end up with your money. I preferred to be asked: "Hersh, can you help me solve this problem?" Being asked seems cleaner, more ethical.

But I was dead wrong in these assumptions. Waiting to be asked is just shirking our responsibility to speak up when we see an opportunity to help someone. I've withheld solutions that were needed by others because I didn't want to "push" anything on them.

What I should have been doing was sharing my solutions with as many people as possible, thus helping their business while building my own. This is what it means to "sell the truth."

This book brings together these two fundamental concepts—selling and being truthful in the process—exploring each in depth, with an acknowledgement of our imperfections. Because truth isn't just something we tell; it's what we believe.

I've learned that each of us must sell daily—a solution, a concept, an image. And often, we must sell to ourselves. In fact, we must sell that thing to ourselves *before* we can sell it to others. And for all the smacking around, stretching, twisting, and concealing we've done with truth, by definition, it is the only thing that remains unbreakable.

So, I decided to put down the insights and strategies that laid the foundation for my own unbreakable truths, which make up my personal "life marketing model." In so doing, I have realized that I must recognize my own truth and embrace it before I can set about selling anything to anyone else.

Without this "knowing," you and I are left to sell without understanding what we're really trying to deliver to others. This book is my attempt at helping you recognize your own "life marketing model" so you can set about selling the truth with great integrity and intention to those you may be able to help in your own circle of influence.

To accomplish this, I'm introducing a new genre of business book: the *semoir* (or "semi-memoir"). I'm not sharing my life story per se, but rather drawing on experiences or impressions that have provided me insight into helping others properly present their brand voice, whether that voice is about their own personal image, a product, service, solution, or idea. One way or another, it all circles back to what is often ignored when pursuing success: reality.

Rather than a "handbook" for branding and business professionals, this is my version of a handy (and hopefully humorous) read about life, business, and brand-building from the inside out. It doesn't matter whether you got here through your interest in business, personal development, or the desire to read a new nonfiction author; the experience of reading *Selling the Truth* will be unique to you. You should come away from this having been moved to take stock of the truth, of reality, of image—especially your own reality and image—and how they are perceived by others, and more importantly, how you perceive them. You should be inspired to approach your personal brand and professional endeavors with a fresh take on "the truth." In fact, I recommend coming to this book with a "get to the next level by getting down with your bad self" attitude.

The chapters in this book represent "Nine Knowings of Selling the Truth," which are not merely *amuseful* (amusing *and* useful), they are foundational, and they're worth keeping close at hand. It has been my experience that by applying these nine principles to your life, your audience will come to better trust and love you.

I liken reading this book to spending some one-on-one time with the truth. If truth were a person, what insights would they offer? How would they help you be a strong servant leader, grow your company, or advance in business? What problems might you have with truth, and how would you address them? How would you come to relate to truth and consider it a trusted partner in your endeavors?

WHO THE H*LL AM I TO AUTHOR THIS BOOK?

Well, for one thing, I'm a writer. I've written three movies (featuring bikinis, martial artists, and Bruce Campbell, in that order); hours of standup comedy; reams of ad copy; and thousands of taglines, titles, bios, press releases, videos, and to-do lists. This is my first book, however, and I'm so pleased that you're experiencing it with me.

For another, this book is a perfect example of what I mean by "selling the truth" because as I noted earlier in this chapter, I am looking inward, digging for what's real about me, what matters to me, and how my strengths and weaknesses function (or don't) as I barrel through my "furious 50s," the age at which we pivot to accomplish all the things we kinda knew we wanted to do, fully recognizing that retirement is not among them.

And for another, over the past three decades, I've been a messaging and media professional, variously handling public relations and marketing for 7- to 9-figure global brands and successful entrepreneurs in the B2B and B2C space. My target audience comprises high achievers at a crossroads, be they my contemporaries or those born around the time I started my career.

I'm also a stand-up comedian. Over the years, I've played the Comedy Cellar, Comic Strip, StandUp NY, Boston Comedy, Broadway Comedy, and Caroline's in New York City; The Comedy Store, Improv, HaHa, Ice House, and Flappers in Los Angeles; and the Funny Bone in Des Moines. I've achieved everything one could possibly achieve as a standup, short of making a living at it.

Finally, I'm a husband, father, and new grandfather, whose hair has not yet turned gray (celebrate those small wins!). I chose fatherhood and family as a young man and even valued how I'd be relatively young as a father-in-law and grandfather. But for many years, I questioned whether I'd missed my opportunity at fame and fortune. Only after becoming a grandfather (being promoted to "Papa") did I realize that I wasn't designed to be a "young star" or even a "star" in the traditional sense, but that my role was championing others, and that "performing" only worked for me as part of a more directly transformational endeavor.

A pivotal player in my relationship with the world, with truth, the presence of humor and humanity in my work, and thus a big influence on my writing is Allan Sherman. Sherman was a satirist, comedian, songwriter, and television producer who broke out as a song parodist in the early 1960s. His first album, *My Son, the Folk Singer*, became the fastest-selling record album up to that time. JFK was heard singing Sherman's "Hello Mudduh, Hello Fadduh" from this album, which hit number 2 on The Billboard Hot 100 and stayed there for three weeks beginning August 24, 1963. The song also won a Grammy in 1964 for Best Comedy Single. Sherman's lampooning of life's absurdity and the social norms we strive to accommodate—poverty, inequity, and the rampant, petty hypocrisies that exist in human relationships—factored into my adoration of him. They also helped shape my own career and the way I have helped shape the careers of others.

All these things—my writing, stand-up comedy, family life, my admiration of Sherman—speak to the path I've taken to gain "qualifications" as the author of this book. As a reader of it, you might reflect on your own path, what you've achieved so far and what worlds you have yet to conquer. And hopefully, the knowings and musings we will explore further in upcoming chapters will provide a new spin (not a doctored one, see *Chapter 4*) on the possibilities that lie before you.

Am I a thought leader? It's not for me to say.

I do believe that we are all leaders at heart, from the youngest and most novice of us, to the most advanced and experienced. And the further we push the boundaries of our abilities—the more we think things through—the better leaders we will be.

If you're not careful, this book will open your mind and arm you with tips for brand building, relationship building, and success (however you define it) in a chaotic world that seems devoid of truth. I'm only partially kidding. Sometimes, we find it challenging to accept ideas and information into our minds. My take is that great advice is what we already know but prefer to ignore until someone points it out to us. For the next hundred-something pages, I'm hoping to be that person, telling you stuff you probably know already, but in a way that makes you want to hear it. I sincerely hope to make you smile through a lot of it, just as I wish for you to smile through much of your life. This is after all, a feel-good book, a book that you should come through feeling good about your chances for success.

Pretty big, huh?

Any lawyers reading this are probably saying, "Don't make a claim like that, you're exposing yourself." I come from a family of lawyers (I'm the black sheep), and I'm proud to say that none of them has ever sued me. Anyway, I'm telling you this stuff to help you, and if I do my job right, when you finish this book, you won't wanna sue *anybody*.

Now, let's do this.

"Legit Bios for Fake People" is something I concocted to engage in a deeper exploration of someone about whom we've made a judgment; they are a means of redefining what we previously thought of as absolute: the truth. I'll begin each chapter with a "Legit Bio" that ties into the topic at hand.

TONY MONTANA
Scarface

For some, the "American Dream" seems unattainable, obstructed by a confluence of obstacles, often the result of hypocrisies woven into the fabric of the country. It is inspiring then, to consider the story of Miami businessman Tony Montana, who came to the United States from Castro's Cuba unafraid of hard work and undaunted by the many steps between his beginnings and the future he dreamed of.

The son of an American father and a Cuban mother, Mr. Montana worked his way up from dishwasher to dealmaker. He was separated from his mother Georgina and younger sister Gina for five long years before making his way to Miami and claiming the green card to which he was entitled given his father's citizenship.

Along with his friend Manolo "Manny" Ribera, Mr. Montana began humbly with a kitchen job. He would soon be reunited with his family and go on to finance his sister's beauty school education, without which she would not have been able to open her salon, Gina's. Mr. Montana's meteoric rise from Little Havana to big business may be due to his unique combination of truthfulness and trustworthiness. "I always tell the truth, even when I lie," he once said at a formal dinner attended by some of Miami's most celebrated community members. This plainspoken style was also on display when he assured a business associate, "I only got two things in this world, my balls and my word. And I don't break 'em for nobody."

Indeed, despite the demands of his multimillion-dollar automotive empire (including Lopez Motors, which he has run since the untimely passing of his friend and mentor, Frank Lopez), Mr. Montana lavishes the most attention on the love of his life, his wife Elvira Hancock. While the couple has no children, Mr. Montana's fascination with wildlife led to the procurement of a pet tiger who resides on the couple's sprawling property. Perhaps the finest testament to Tony Montana's American Dream is the centerpiece of his palatial home: a statue of three women holding up a globe carrying the inscription "The World Is Yours."

᷍

This Legit Bio for Tony Montana—from Brian De Palma's 1983 crime thriller, *Scarface*—is delivered with a wink, of course. I am leaving out key details that would round out the picture. I do this to demonstrate that there are no alternative facts, only alternative narratives. And each narrative is supported by a certain perspective. As we set about "selling the truth," fact and perspective will bump up against each other. My hope is to reconcile the two in a paradigm shift for personal and corporate brands alike because life and business are easier and more fruitful when we work with what we have instead of what others wish were true.

CHAPTER 1:

SELLING THE TRUTH

I love that authenticity has become a thing. Every time I hear how "Gen L" (my name for whatever the *latest* generation is called) "craves authenticity," I wonder if the implication is that all previous generations were simply hungry for bullshit. I do think it's reasonable to observe that the past decade has been globally polarizing in that we have flung to one of two extremes: obsessed with bullshit or obsessed with reality. Whether we call it a post-truth world or an era of relative truth, as a society, we no longer agree about what's real and what's fantasy. So, how do we "sell the truth" to our audience when they may have a different definition of what's true?

Big, scary question, right? But here's the good news: Establishing mutual trust with your audience is possible, even when "truth" has become so hard to agree upon. You just have to develop a new litmus test for reality.

The first order of business in creating this test is to accept that even in today's world, not all truth is relative—this is the first of the

Nine Knowings we will explore in this book—and the fact is, simple facts are truly discoverable.

KNOWING NO. 1: NOT ALL TRUTH IS RELATIVE

For example, if you stub your toe, and you register intense, sudden pain that causes you to release a string of swear words—that's real. That happened. If you come down for breakfast, and you are out of your favorite cereal—that's a fact.

Here's another fact, from my life:

I grew up in Florida. I crave the ocean, and viewing the horizon over glimmering water fuels my spirit. I loved living in Florida, and I relished my twenty years in Los Angeles. Yet, for the past eight years, I have lived in Iowa. Now, there are reasons for and benefits to this. However, I cannot change the past, so those eight years are not up for discussion, regardless of how I feel about them—the truth is not dependent on my likes and dislikes. No degree of rationalization will change reality. Accepting what is allows the greatest amount of hope to influence the future. I can take action today and change the story for tomorrow, but that cannot happen until I accept the past.

So, what do these three examples of reality have in common?

- Evidence
- Simplicity
- Frustration

The first two in this list are the operative ones, but it's interesting that frustration is also such a big part of our reality. So, if we are going to try to isolate the truth away from relativity, we not only need simple, fact-based evidence, we also must accept that we are going to bump up against frustration along the way...

...Regardless of who moved the couch or turned out the light.

...No matter who finished the cereal.

...Apart from what we want tomorrow to look like.

But no matter how frustrating things might be, we must begin relearning the truth by discovering facts for which the evidence is simple. These may not be the hot button issues of our day, but before we come to the negotiating table on truth, we need to brush up on reality.

I propose we start with those examples that are closest to our personal experience. Am I sitting on a chair right now? Do I really accept the rationalizations for my current geographical placement? How much money did my business bring in last month? How is my brand really perceived by my audience? We must get back to basics. We must *relearn* the truth.

As I noted in the Introduction, truth can taste funny if we aren't used to experiencing it. We have become so confused by our tenuous tether to reality that AI now threatens to take over our lives. We are terrified of being vulnerable—reality has become too big and scary and the mirror too hard to look in.

Fear of the truth, since much of our truth has become so massively overwhelming, is what makes it essential for us to start with simple, evidence-based facts. Again, we must *relearn* truth so we can stop being afraid of it, face it, embrace it, look in the mirror instead of pretending we aren't who we are, and that our business is not what it is, and that our brands aren't what they are. As noted in the last chapter, we must befriend truth and enlist it in our endeavors, both personal and professional.

For me, that's meant creating a new "life marketing model" based on simple facts about my life. Over the past few months, those facts have included stubbing my toe on the couch seven times, running out of my favorite cereal twice, and wondering, almost every day, why we don't just pick up and move to a tropical locale.

These are basic truths, simple facts I have kept track of daily. I have also kept track of the fact that in the past year, I have worked with numerous coaches on various aspects of my business, attended a four-day immersion to get the most out of my meditation practice, and used humor often to help sell truth in my work as a communicator. The results of these endeavors are subjective. But the fact is, I've taken these steps.

As you keep track of the simple truths about yourself, your brand, your product, and your voice, you will have the power to begin building the foundation for a better, more fruitful relationship with your audience, clients, business partners, associates, and even your own family.

Another thing this "simple accounting of the truth" accomplishes is to help you swim where you can tread water instead of drowning in the sea of "truth is relative" nonsense. For example, social media is a wicked shitshow that's pretty easy to get bogged down in. Even though there's a steady flow of data, there seems to be very little reality within it. These social media apps feel somewhat like a murky swimming hole, where we tend to be drawn into the deepest, darkest parts, awash in a swirling haze of muck of our own making: we state, overstate, and restate the obvious, and we do verbal battle with one another from politics to entertainment to everything in between. But to what end? Our species appears predisposed to hanging out in muddy waters, where simple facts are hard to come by, instead of swimming to clearer pools where we can see our own feet where we can keep track of the simple facts, where we can make an actual accounting of what really matters. We complicate things.

And no, by saying social media is a shit show, I'm not making a moral judgment, despite how insidious and ill-intended some of the people behind these apps are, and what they are doing to our kids (see *The Social Dilemma* on Netflix). After all, you and I, no doubt, use social media to help run our businesses, right? The fact is, I'm on Instagram and Facebook, and I had a TikTok account. The only thing I feel good about is LinkedIn (although in addition to being a great platform for professional networking, it does seem to serve as a "Facebook for retirees" so there's that).

The point is, even a wicked shitshow has a silver lining.

While I'm ashamed of the time I spent trying to be clever or snide on Facebook and Twitter between 2015 and 2020, those apps, which I used more deliberately during the pandemic, served as a wakeup call for me and the catalyst for discovering the more basic, simple truths about myself and my own personal brand. For instance, during lockdown, I used Instagram to create a new account called 3xDailyComedy, where I posted a few silly character videos each day to provide the requisite dose of humor required (for me, anyway) to survive 2020 and 2021. I think I posted something like 300 videos. Many featured my younger kids and the journey we took into our imaginations while bumping up against the frustration of an uncertain reality.

Since the pandemic triggered an internal reaction to the news, where we all felt like the Four Horsemen might be parking their steeds up our asses, the truth was, we needed a spoonful of humor to get all that "news" down. The 3xDailyComedy posts were my way of swimming to where I could tread and getting back to the basics of my own truth—which is that humor is a powerful way to sell the truth! I'll talk a lot about comedy in this book, mostly in the context of how it can work for you and your business—it's an amazing icebreaker, tension-easer, and sanity-saver. That said, it's important to know yourself before wielding this tool. Comedy is as powerful as Thor's hammer. And I'm sure he smashed his toe more than once before learning how to throw that damn thing.

The humorous videos—the product of my attempts to escape the clutches of the fake social media world when COVID was a thing—became a springboard for helping others discover more reality in their own lives. These videos also laid the foundation for the launch of my *Truth Tastes Funny* podcast.

In May of 2022, I was approached by Kyle Sullivan of Pantheon. FM's *The Lucky Titan* podcast about launching my own show. He and Lucky Titan creator, Josh Tapp, were putting together a network of "one thousand of the world's best humans" and invited me to join the team. Sticking with my theme-in-progress, I launched a podcast called *Truth Tastes Funny* about staying sane, surviving, and thriving in an absurd, chaotic world. With the guidance of Pantheon.FM, I set about creating the podcast, doing all the work myself—tech, recording, editing, outreach—all of it.

While we shared laughs in the face of reality, the podcast attracted guests dealing with the heaviest topics: addiction, suicide, abuse, PTSD… and this was in the first 10 episodes! I wasn't sure that I was equipped to conduct these interviews. That's how I knew I was onto something. I categorized *Truth Tastes Funny* as a "personal development" podcast instead of a "comedy" podcast. In its first nine months, the show crossed 50,000 downloads, ranking in the Top 2 percent of podcasts globally, according to ListenNotes. Apparently, that's good.

Since I had not constructed a business model around *Truth Tastes Funny*, I had the freedom to do with it what I wished. This was a blessing because my only allegiance was to each guest—to make sure I was serving them and honoring their purpose—and to the audience we would attract together. Nine months, some really nice reviews, and nearly 10,000 monthly downloads later, I realized that all the while, without monetizing this show at all, I was getting back to the basics of who I really am as a communicator and brand builder. I was relearning the simple truths about myself and my ability to sell the truth, and I was *building my brand*. Not a comedy brand. Not a self-help brand. Not a brand messaging brand. Not an entertainment brand. A *Hersh* brand. I was "selling the truth," even if I was giving it away. I didn't worry about which box I fit into. I built my own box to fit my persona like a glove. I dived deep into the process of finding myself, and it was truly liberating (more on that to come in the next chapter!).

So, the takeaway from this chapter may be that while we cannot control external realities or perceptions; truth is not relative (Knowing No. 1), and is, in fact, quite discoverable. As Tony Montana reminds us, all we really have are our balls (or similar) and our word. These are the simple truths about life... let them speak volumes about who we really are.

Onward!

NURSE MILDRED RATCHED
One Flew Over the Cuckoo's Nest

Rather than treat her patients as numbers or names on a chart, Mildred Ratched, head administrative nurse at Salem State Hospital, knows the quirks and proclivities of each and every one. From disruptive patients, like Randle Patrick McMurphy (Antisocial Personality Disorder), to Billy Bibbit (Generalized Anxiety Disorder)—whose mother Mildred speaks to regularly, providing updates on her son's progress—she is cognizant of them all.

For many, the vision of a psychiatric treatment center is one in which patients are viewed as a problem. And yet, it is astounding to watch Mildred maintain her composure in the face of uproarious behavior, including such rebellious acts as an unauthorized bus ride and the smuggling of illegal substances and visitors into the ward. Make no mistake: Mildred does not suffer fools, nor does she believe licentiousness is the path toward healing. Rather, she fosters a spirit of meritocracy, rewarding patients for their adherence to the rules, and ensuring that infractions will be answered with consequences, just as they would be in the outside world. It is worth pointing out that, while not every inmate is pleased with the system, some patients remain in the hospital on a voluntary basis, testimony to the touch of this singular caregiver, one with no known equal in the nursing profession.

⤚

Nurse Ratched, who sprung from the mind of novelist Ken Kesey and whose character was portrayed with terrifying precision by Louis Fletcher in the 1975 film, is unflappable because she knows her brand (both she and Jack Nicholson as McMurphy, won Best Acting Oscars for their performances). There is no confusion around her purpose. This makes her hard to break, but Kesey's counter character, Randle McMurphy—likewise committed to his brand—succeeds. It's a battle to the death: she lives, but he wins.

CHAPTER 2

BEFORE YOU BRAND YOURSELF, KNOW YOURSELF

✦

The truth I want to begin this chapter with is that *you* are a brand name, whether you know it or not. To be a success as a business leader, at branding your company and products, and in selling the truth to those in search of it...you must know yourself.

Some people bristle at the use of the word "brand" in describing themselves because it implies commercialization of one's persona, akin to selling one's soul. Others feel it confers a label upon them.

But what does it mean, really, to be branded?

Let me try to answer that question by first going way back to the Old English and Germanic definitions of *brand:*

Old English: brond, "fire, flame, destruction by fire; firebrand, piece of burning wood, torch.

Proto-Germanic: brandaz, "a burning."

From these definitions, people may have the idea that branding is a mark or a stamp. Of course, commercial branding has its origins based in this definition, and the idea also comes from ranchers using such stamps to "brand" their name into the hide of their cattle. But in the business world, we must look at branding as more than just stamping our name on a product. It's not just a mark, a logo, or even a name. These components may make up the brand's elements, but they aren't the brand itself. According to legendary copywriter and advertising agency founder, David Ogilvy, branding is defined as "the intangible sum of a product's attributes—its name, packaging and price, its history, its reputation, and the way it's advertised."

So, your personal brand is the intangible sum of all your attributes, including your name, the way you present yourself, what kind of perceived value you bring to the table, your background and history, your reputation, and most importantly, your individual way of selling the truth, both about yourself and the products and services over which you have responsibility.

I advocate for this personalization of our core attributes because my work as a communicator is about deeply connecting with all the facets of the human condition and exploring the farthest reaches of the mortal imagination. No matter how technical your product or service, or how scientific your thinking, understanding the personal spark of individuality behind what you offer others is what drives your ability to sell the truth.

When working with clients or interviewing guests on podcasts, I zero in on the spark of individuality behind each person to make a connection with them that will help them get to the truth of whatever it is we're exploring together.

This spark is at once everything and nothing. I'll use myself as an example: I have, in the past, underestimated myself and my own spark, struggling to compensate for a perceived lack of accomplishment and associating dollars earned with effort expended. I thought I was a lazy dreamer. What I really am is a hyper-achiever, who attained the things that mattered to me (family, friendships, professional integrity) while eschewing or avoiding material rewards until I felt worthy of them.

There's more to cover regarding the usefulness of self-discovery, but first, I want to share another reason why homing in on your individual brand is so important: individuality leads to originality.

FIND YOURSELF (AND YOUR ORIGINALITY) ... BEFORE YOU LOSE YOUR PHONE!

I've attended the Cannes Lions advertising festival (now known as the Festival of Creativity) in the South of France 13 times. I have only lost my phone there twice, and once I got it back (so, all things considered, I'm pretty good at rationalization). I've lost my phone in many other places as well—Las Vegas (four times, got it back once, so a 25 percent success rate!), Miami (once), and Los Angeles (found once, that's what counts!). Why? Alcohol was the trigger, but not the cause. I lost my phone because I relinquished control. I did that because I was uncertain about who I was and what I wanted. Had I "known myself" during those periods in my life, my phone would have remained securely in my possession.

The same is true of your brand. If you know who you are and what you mean to stand for and accomplish, you will not get lost.

Not only that, but your audience will know that you are selling the truth and be willing to follow you for your originality, for what you can offer them in terms of discovering their own individuality. After all, certainty is contagious.

The more thoroughly you consider and test your own idea of yourself, the more efficiently you can tell your story (and in the case of hiring a professional communicator such as myself, the more they can help you tell your story across all platforms). Because quite frankly, the individual that you are is the most important and most convincing part of you. This leads to the second Knowing I want to share with you:

KNOWING NO. 2: BEFORE YOU CAN BRAND YOURSELF, YOU HAVE TO KNOW YOURSELF

How can you come to know yourself more intimately?

First, keep your eyes open wide. What does this mean? I'll give you an example from my own life to illustrate.

To build a healthy relationship with the truth, I had to admit that reality scares me. I had to open my eyes to my fears. What was I afraid of? We'll talk about epigenetic imprinting later, but I now believe the trauma carried by my ancestors—as recently as my father's grandparents, cousins, and other relatives who were murdered in the Holocaust—made an indelible mark on my soul. Despite an idyllic childhood in Miami Beach, I sought to escape into fantasy, into comedy, and into characters. With an ear for voices, dialects, and behaviors, I am a natural actor and comedian. The trauma was not always visible to the naked eye (nor is it unusual among Jews post-WWII), so I assumed this was all about talent and the imperative I felt to use it, to make a career of it. But that's only half the story.

I've discovered that while my early screenplays and comedy were pretty thin, they were in line with my own evaluation of myself, that I was deeply entertaining but intellectually superficial. I've since learned that conclusion was false. My purpose lay not in evading the truth but rather in unmasking it, revealing it, and most importantly, surviving it.

Better late than next Thursday.

The second strategy for knowing yourself more intimately is not to cling to the perceptions of your youth. These perceptions are formed as early as 2 to 7 years, where research shows the reason kids often have their "heads in the clouds." Children aged 2 to 7 years are typically in the theta brainwave state, where creativity, intuition, daydreaming, and fantasizing roam free. From 7 to 12 years, a child's brain enters the alpha state, where it can absorb new information with ease and can be significantly more creative. After approximately 12 years, we move into the beta brainwave. This is the area of conscious thought and logical thinking. The right amount of beta waves allows us to focus. This focus is great for fast-tracking cognitive learning, but it's also a way to ensure that things get boring real quick. Being an adult with a fully developed pre-frontal cortex has always been at odds with my "childhood dreams." I should have seen these dreams as foundational, not to be taken literally, but I did not really know myself or what I should aspire to as an adult.

At the age of 7, when I was in the alpha brainwave state, still with my head in the clouds, I stood beside the piano in our house, holding one of my sister's recital prizes (a small bust of Bach, if I remember correctly), and delivered my Oscar acceptance speech. Everything after that is a blur. Kind of. I have no idea what I said, or whether the award was for Best Actor or Best Supporting Actor (my recent performance as the Scarecrow in our second-grade production of *The Wizard of Oz* would have earned me a Supporting nomination). Somehow, in some parts of my life, I got stuck in this alpha state, thinking—because I had acting, performing, and creative talent that had not gone unnoticed by others around me—that the only way to success would be to go undeviatingly down that road. I saw it as my life's purpose instead of a foundation for all the creativity that I was meant to exhibit even amongst the "boring" bits of beta brainwaves I thought I would have to "endure" in adulthood. That was 50 years ago. If I were to give that speech today, it would go something like this:

"The first day of rehearsal as the Scarecrow, I showed up having memorized the entire script. That's how committed I was to the craft of acting. And here I am, accepting this incredible honor. I thank you from the bottom of my heart, because in some alternate universe, I'm merely standing in front of a piano, speaking into the mirror, giving a speech I will never give, for a job I'll never do.

Because I'm too scared...

Scared of disappointing my parents by making art more important than G-d.

Scared of betting on myself.

Scared of failing.

Scared of losing what I already have.

Scared of finding out that there are limitations to my talent.

Scared of declaring that I am unique.

Scared of going all in.

Instead, I'll spend the years between my Bar Mitzvah and its Jubilee...

Writing screenplays (screenwriters don't have to work on the Sabbath; actors do),

Creating a niche in PR and copywriting,

Disappointing my family,

Working on the Sabbath,

Performing standup comedy,

Co-creating a purpose-driven streetwear brand,

Developing a fresh take on brand strategy,

Writing this book,

Having incredible kids,

Finding an awesome partner,

Raising a beautiful family,

Becoming a grandfather,

Finding myself,

And finally, realizing that my dreams as a kid were nowhere nearly as exciting as the reality of my life as it has unfolded and how rewarding, creative, challenging, and wonderfully difficult it has all been.

Wait, wait, don't play me off. I've been waiting a long time for this. Thing is…I can't accept this Oscar, because, uh, it might mean giving up some of that other stuff that happened. And because, you know…this isn't a real Oscar."

The instructive element here is the fact that from age 7, I held on to a vision of myself as an actor and even the compromises (screenwriting, standup comedy) were outgrowths of that vision. I did not fully accept the natural evolution of my brain wave states. This, in and of itself, doesn't have to be a problem, but in my case, it slowed my development. It confused my maturation process. I have just enough talent, skill, and dedication to make progress in an area like show business. But success as an entertainer requires dedication beyond simple movement. It takes precedence over any other goal or life choice, including the really important stuff like family and faith. They all must take a back seat. As you can see from my acceptance speech, this really important stuff was a priority, and it was stuff that came forth in alpha and beta states.

So, this tip for knowing yourself is both negative and positive: don't ignore your own growth as you mature, thinking you are "giving up" on your foundational childhood dreams. But do account for your personal development and check in with yourself more throughout your life (and, ideally, read this book at age 7.)

A third strategy for knowing yourself is to look at the playing field from 30,000 feet, and don't flinch. Objectivity is hard to achieve, but it's our friend. I dream almost every night, multiple times, and I suspect there's a reason why our dreams sometimes possess this odd quality of first-person and third-person identification, meaning we can at once see ourselves and be inside ourselves looking out. Pull away from your life for a few moments each day to objectively view your place in the world. Look at the world in its enormity and what exists around you, beyond the self. That's fancy for "don't be a schmuck."

Finally, catch up to those ahead of you long enough for them to assess your potential. Their opinion matters (see *Chapter 5* on third-party validation).

If I could change anything, it wouldn't necessarily be that I never became a famous actor or entertainer (who was worthy of an Oscar and making that speech for real). What I would change would be to go easier on myself in those 50 years. I would have allowed myself to be happier sooner, and I would have acknowledged and loved myself for what I chose to do, instead of what I thought I was supposed to do. The best I can do now is to acknowledge that I *didn't* love myself, and that it was not okay. But at least I *know* this now...and that has helped me brand myself in the most authentic of ways.

Why am I telling you this? What do fear, faith, family, excuses, timing, maturity, personal development and mindset have to do with finding and knowing yourself so you can create effective messaging and brand awareness, so you can ultimately sell the truth?

...Exactly.

My conscious self-discovery is an evolution that advanced greatly during the pandemic with my *Truth Tastes Funny* podcast. For that podcast I took steps—not all of them linear—to finally, after years of trying to be at least two things at any given moment (comedian/copywriter, publicist/screenwriter, father/sex symbol), refine and define *myself.* I had no plan for this. Typically, I would go where the writing work was, falling back into standup, screenwriting, even music when the work dried up, believing that my creative aptitude would sweep me out of the doldrums and into the rarefied atmosphere where entertainers and actors earn a living. What I was really doing was distracting myself instead of innovating a path through the business challenges I was facing.

But during this time, I successively threw into the mix a Peak Performance workshop, meditation, podcasting, community-building, mastermind classes, along with quantum consciousness acceleration. Consider it a cosmic way to break bad habits, love yourself, and welcome into your life what's "missing" (or what you're blocking). I started doing things I didn't love in the service of capitalizing on the things I genuinely enjoyed.

In short, I began finding myself.

And the self I discovered was not new—he'd been there all along. Like Dorothy's Kansas, I had been in my own backyard. This self was bigger than a job title, or career, or money, and he lunged in one direction only, the disjointed dabbling set aside for things of a more purposeful nature. It was there that I accepted what I do, and I think do very well for my clients: listening wholeheartedly to their personal branding truths so I can provide what I call "MESSAGE Therapy." This therapy helps them sell the truth more effectively to their audience. During this therapy, they realize that truth has been tasting a little funny because, you know, they aren't necessarily used to it. But then I show them how good it can feel to really find themselves, and oh how sweet truth becomes for my clients, and for me as well, when we finally savor it in all its sumptuousness.

During all this, I managed to come across many, many colleagues—who, like me—suffered from imposter syndrome. There are many causes of this phenomenon, but in my case, what I perceived as modesty gave way to self-deprecation and minimization. Not good. Or necessary. Because, you know, while humility is integral to a healthy self-image, you don't need to suppress your self-confidence, assertiveness, presence, or potential. If you work hard enough to convince people that you suck, eventually it will take. Everyone has superpowers; own yours and bury the bullshit and negative self-talk in a shoe box in the backyard.

These are the kinds of conversations I have with clients. Because if you're able to get real about yourself, your brands and business models have a shot at winning your customers' trust and getting to the next level.

YOUR CUSTOMERS AREN'T FOR SALE

Customers can buy your product, but their loyalty is not so easily acquired. So, before you try to sell them anything, consider the relationship you want to build with your audience, a relationship that only comes by getting real with yourself, by finding your purpose, by knowing *you*.

If customer loyalty matters…

If authenticity is a thing…

If we're building relationships with our audiences…

…Then we have to get real with ourselves, face the mirror, sit with our fears, look at the problems, and stop numbing ourselves with distractions within our businesses and virtual realities. As we continue to be mined for data, the companies that initiate such activities are buying us as customers. But they don't give a shit about us. They sell us to other brands, and we don't even know it. Sheesh, I spend more time hiding ads and telling Instagram I'm "not interested" than I do utilizing content on the platform. But can I get off the platform? Should I abandon it, or stay and use it for good instead of evil? Sure, my relationship with Mark Zuckerberg sucks. But I can't quit his apps. What I can do is try to lay the foundation for a healthier brand-consumer relationship with my own clients than I currently have with him and all the social media rapscallions I am forced to do business with in the Information Age. My personal brand can take a different approach to those I have vowed to sell the truth. I prefer to take the attitude that over the life of our business together, my client and I will have a beautiful and very real and personal friendship.

OUR CHOICES REFLECT OUR BRAND

Sometimes, in our even more intentional efforts to find our true self, instead of asking why we are doing what we're doing, we should reflect a little on why we've done what we've done. I've spent much of my life telling the stories behind the creation of outstanding advertising campaigns, and clearly have a fondness for the medium. There must be a reason why—despite my affinity for clever turns of phrase—I didn't become an agency copywriter.

No matter where you land, whether you sell your product door-to-door, online, in stores, on the street, or by helping others sell their products and get their message out, you are forming a business relationship with each and every customer. That relationship is based on your personal brand, which is based on a promise. We've talked a lot up to this point about what branding is and is not, but we haven't really addressed the most important aspect of branding, which in its purest form is a promise. The messages you use to market yourself or your business communicate that promise, and your personal reputation or product is the fulfillment of that promise.

If you're going to make, convey, and keep promises, you must upend the misperception around brand image, both personal and corporate, and set the stage for a paradigm of selling the truth.

This chapter has been about personal branding, and the role it plays in selling the truth, regardless of our overt efforts to "brand" our products and services. We've also touched on building relationships that hold value based on knowing who we really are and staying true to that understanding.

So, hopefully, this notion of selling the truth is starting to take greater shape. (You did it, didn't you? You jumped right to the end of this chapter to see what the summary is! Okay, but if you're a "skipper" or a "skimmer," it's my hope that you will go back now and give this chapter a closer look and meet me back here later.)

Okay, in the next chapter, we will look at what happens to our ability to sell the truth when we lie to ourselves, which is a natural follow on to everything we have explored in this chapter on personal branding. We have a lot more to cover but suffice it to say we are now two Knowings down, with only seven to go!

THE WICKED WITCH OF THE WEST
The Wizard of Oz
(a first-person account delivered via email)

Hey Hersh!

You said I should just riff, so here's my Monday morning brain dump:

They say you can call yourself anything you want, but your name is what other people call you. That's turned out to be true because while I could say "Elphaba Throp" a thousand times in a row, when I'm banging around the Winkie Country I'm going to hear, "Hey, that's The Wicked Witch of the West!" All I can tell you is pejorative labels don't make anyone a better person.

It doesn't matter which country you live in, people can be cruel, especially to an aquaphobe with blotchy skin. What I wish people would see is the human behind the broomstick. The Wizard of Oz himself has been after that stick for ages, and who can blame him—it flies! Cool! But take away the broom, the golden cap, the crystal ball, and the other magical affectations, and all I am is a woman. A woman who's suffered loss and carried on.

My sister, Nessarose, was the only one who really got me. They called her "The Wicked Witch of the East" (soooo creative). She was killed by a troubled young girl from another planet, who stole her slippers (whaaa?). That alone should have sent me to therapy, but the closest thing to mental healthcare they have around here is the spa in the Emerald City (they're hardly ever open, and I can't go there anyway, long story).

So, under the protection of Glinda, the "Good Witch of the North" (so a "good" witch encourages theft, now?), this kid Dorothy is making me chase her all over the place to try to reclaim my inheritance. This craziness has taken me away from my central pursuit, caring for a rare breed of

Cercopithecoidea, otherwise known as "winged monkeys" (remember what I said earlier about names). I'd really like my bio to be more about that stuff, and the 40 wolves I care for. The humanitarian side of my life. I also have welcomed a tribe of local single men to live with me in my castle (don't get the wrong idea, I've never seen them out of uniform), who march around in a daze carrying spears. Can you tell I'm lonely?

The closest I've come to dating lately has been my encounter with a scarecrow, a tin woodsman, and a lion who talks, sings, and is afraid of his own tail. Getting my hands on some magic slippers doesn't sound like the craziest idea ever right about now.

So. Do you think you can turn this into a decent bio? Or maybe a Q&A is better? You're the expert!

Xoxo,

E-phab

&

Frank L. Baum's *The Wonderful Wizard of Oz* was first published in 1900 and made into the 1939 spectacular epic, *The Wizard of Oz*, starring Judy Garland. For this bio, I brought Baum's character of The Wicked Witch of the West into today's world. It's fun to turn a fantastic, indelible image on its ear. But there's more to it than that. With this email, Elphaba (I'll call her "E-phab" just for fun) normalizes her behavior. E-phab is friendly and breezy and tries to convince us that nothing she does is all that serious.

But she is, in fact, lying to herself, and trying to put one over on us as well—of course, we know that she will soon attempt to murder Dorothy and reclaim the ruby slippers to wield their power for her evil pursuits. We see a lot of "normalization" like hers these days, a lot of manipulation in the business, enterprise leadership, and branding space. And thus, we are susceptible, more than ever, to self-delusion.

CHAPTER 3

A LIE IS A WISH YOUR HEART MAKES

❖

I first performed stand-up comedy 35 years ago, and let me tell you, it can be brutal. That's because if you want your audience to find you funny you've got to get savagely honest with yourself, and, frankly, with them as well. You gotta lean into the discomfort, be cool with exposing yourself. Nothing funny comes from lying to yourself—after all, there's nothing more hilarious than the truth. And all of us can relate to it.

My brother-in-comedy, Justo Diaz, urged me to use some of that brutal honesty in my comedy act, so I wove in some pretty heavy-hitting material—things like getting a DUI in 2009, for instance, and admitting I've had suicidal ideations. Of course, there's no need to go into details here other than to tell you that including such material forever changed my approach to standup, public speaking, and performing as a whole. It not only elevated my comedy, but it was also cathartic and laid the groundwork for selling the truth in business and life.

That honesty helped me face the truth about myself with less fear because humor is, after all, the way we help others stomach the truth, truth that for some time now has tasted rather funny. It's hard to lie when you're making other people laugh—precisely because they see the truth about themselves in your confessions.

I'm not saying you need to perform your confessions like I do. I just propose that you open yourself more to your own truths— stop lying to yourself. That's what this chapter's all about. Start with yourself (and work your way outward) to admit what you are ashamed of or uncomfortable about—this will make it real for you. If you're keeping some truths from yourself, some lessons you need to learn, fessing up opens the door to self-honesty and allows you to question your identity, your purpose, and your brand. Confronting reality is a gateway to selling the truth.

KNOWING NO. 3: YOU CAN'T SELL THE TRUTH WHILE LYING TO YOURSELF

In the last chapter, we explored how important it is to know (find) yourself so you can build your personal brand, and the role that plays in selling the truth. This chapter takes that premise further, confronting self-deception, which is a common stumbling block in any effort to be truthful with others.

A LITTLE TRANSLUCENT LIE

There are all kinds of lies. Not all are malicious. In addition to the perennial white lie to spare someone's feelings, there are lies we tell ourselves. I call these translucent lies because we can almost see through them: we just don't wanna. We can see the shape of the truth on the other side of the glass if we will only look—usually we don't.

We could also call this "mismanifestation." We mistakenly believe that if we tell the lie to ourselves convincingly enough, it will become fact. Again, I'm not referring to malevolent, external disinformation, which, as we have been discussing throughout this book, is a manipulation based on known untruths spread for the benefit of conscious deceivers (more on this in the next chapter). I'm talking about something even more dangerous because you may not even be conscious of it. As such, it creates a hamster wheel of delusion. And because we come to believe our lie, it changes us; we become someone who refuses to accept reality. After all, if reality is relative, why accept one we don't like? And so, our entire existence can come to challenge unimpeachable fact. We become desensitized to reason, and the "little" lie we accepted as fact metastasizes into an open license to change our perception of truth, based not on logic but on wishfulness. Rationalization becomes the order of the day, and we get so used to it that we no longer even distinguish between fact and fiction when it comes to certain subjects. Here's an example.

I am not a licensed psychologist. But in rereading the last paragraph, it sounds like something a licensed psychologist might write. The translucent lie I tell myself is that if I had gone on to study psychology and earned an advanced degree, I could have become a licensed psychologist. After authoring another article that I consider profound and insightful, I reflect on the fact that "psychologist," by definition, is "an expert or specialist in psychology."

"That's me!" I tell myself. "For 30 years, I've been dealing with personalities and their psyches, putting in well over 10,000 hours...

clients, associates, parents, siblings, *five* kids, and an ex-wife! If *I'm* not an expert in psychology, no one is!"

So, I start peppering my book with phrases like, "Psychologically speaking," and "the psychology of sales and marketing," which morphs into "I have drawn on my experience in psychology," and "As any psychologist knows…"

Eventually, I revisit my bio…

"A brand voice expert and psychologist, Hersh Rephun…," it now begins. The word, "psychologist" looks a little lonely, a little spare. I open my mind, noting that the entire university system and post-graduate business is kind of a scam. We've seen pilots and surgeons who did a remarkable job with no formal training, and certainly no "degree." Since we began this chapter with a Legit Bio from *The Wizard of Oz*, it occurs to me that the "Wizard" confers a degree (Th.D., "doctor of thinkology") upon the Scarecrow, delivers a testimonial to the Tin Man, and gives the Cowardly Lion a medal. To my knowledge, none of these characters has ever gone to college, but each has earned their honor. And the Wizard, despite all his fakery, displays profound wisdom and tenderness. If I'd been a character in that story, the Wizard might have given me my Psy.D there and then!

"Psy.D" is formal, it's part of the system I reject, whereas having license to do something is more personal. I tweak the bio: "A brand voice expert and licensed psychologist, Hersh Rephun…,"

By the time I go on tour with my second book, I've become increasingly comfortable doing interviews, and hearing the above description, so much so that I don't even think about it anymore.

And so it goes…

We indulge in this kind of translucent lying to ourselves for all kinds of reasons. It starts in childhood with the compulsion to please our parents (even rebellious kids want to please their parents, and often, their rebellion is born of a sense of failure: if I can't please them, I'll defy them!). We lie to ourselves to avoid making tough decisions. And let's not forget, sometimes we lie because we don't know what's true.

FEAR: OUR BIGGEST REASON FOR LYING TO OURSELVES

Fear, it turns out, was what derailed me for a time, until I called it on the carpet. That fear started early for me. It had me telling myself a bunch of translucent lies, lies that held me bound, preventing me from going on the road as a comedian when I was offered the opportunity for major representation.

First, I feared disappointing family. Becoming an entertainer would mean putting standup ahead of my commitments to Orthodox Judaism and Sabbath observance, and that was something I wasn't sure I wanted to do. And I certainly wasn't prepared to disappoint my family in that way.

Second, I feared failure. If I set out as a comedian and didn't enjoy breakout success, I would have to face a real limit to my talent, the reality that I wasn't as good as I thought I was.

Both of these are bullshit excuses. They are driven by fear, and fear is never a reason, it's a blocker. The truth is I wasn't ready to welcome prosperity into my life with open arms. So, I spent 20 years getting everything half-right—which, if you're a math genius like me—means I also got everything half-wrong.

Why wasn't I ready for prosperity? I didn't know myself. I thought I did; I had put myself in the "artist" basket, assuming this was my entire personality and that the struggle was circumstantial—I never questioned my "destiny" as an actor, comedian, and screenwriter. The struggle I saw before me was between my destiny and my commitments to faith and family. As such, who's to blame for the conflict? Certainly, not me. G-d made me this way. Surely, He had a resolution to this conflict, right?

I reasoned that He'd blessed me with an abundance of writing talent as a means of entering the Hollywood fray, where I would achieve success. From there, I could launch projects for myself to star in. Really. I believed that. Looking back, the notion that G-d gives a shit about Hollywood and screenwriting is ridiculous. Movies would be so much better, in fact, if the Almighty *did* lend a hand (although Michael Cimino's *Heaven's Gate*—considered the biggest box office bomb of all time—is nowhere near as bad as reputed). The core lie I told myself was this: "I am an artist, and as such, I am not equipped to take responsibility for my business success—my true value is in my ability to entertain. The missing pieces are the agents, managers, and producers who stand to profit by exploiting my gifts."

And that's what I thought was my destiny, so much so that it usurped my free-will for a while.

Perhaps you've also done this to yourself at times. As an exercise in awareness, think about your "destiny" for a moment:

1. Do you have one?
2. What is it?
3. On what set of beliefs is it based?
4. What steps are you taking to fulfill it?
5. Who is in control of it?
6. Is your destiny negotiable?

This is a good exercise for each of us to do, because it allows for honest introspection. Questions 5 and 6 are particularly useful. To say that we are not in control of our destiny is to admit defeat as a human being. It's a rejection of free will. And if destiny is not negotiable—meaning we cannot influence the eventual outcome—what are we doing here?

If I had left some doors open in my mind, I might have explored other parts of my personality and investigated my other gifts (see *Chapter 8)*, instead of setting only audacious goals and attempting to accomplish them ASAP.

Speaking to exactly what I did wrong with all my audacious goalsetting, David Asarnow, founder of Business Nitrogen, among other 7-figure businesses, had this to say on my "Brand Voice Runway" podcast: "I don't believe in New Year's resolutions. I believe in setting the plan, implementing that plan, and adjusting that plan on a daily and monthly basis because our minds change, and the fact of the matter is most resolutions don't work. If we set a big goal for ourselves, and we're halfway through it, and we haven't even scratched the surface, then unconsciously our mind doesn't believe that we're going to be able to achieve it. So, we have to chunk it down into smaller, achievable objectives."

But I couldn't bring myself to do that—to knock down my "destiny" goal just a bit, into more reasonable bite-size chunks—for a very long time. I was hell-bent on one thing, and I told myself lies about why I couldn't achieve it. I failed to investigate other possibilities, other amazingly beautiful facets, other truths I could be selling about myself, because I was fearful of the facts I might uncover. I wanted to believe that I had a destiny in "show business." After all, I did have talent and skills and was typically encouraged in my travels. But my vision was too narrow. I used too few of my overall resources.

And you? What fears are now coming to the surface? What lies have you been telling yourself that you now need to fess up to?

Here's the real throughline: fear is tied directly to our current state of confusion over truth, and we lie when we are afraid. So, if we reduce fear, we open the door to more honest communication between ourselves and our audiences, customers, clients, and teams.

DON'T LIE TO YOURSELF, *LIKE* YOURSELF

I just shared some thoughts on free will versus destiny, so now I'd like to touch on personality and identity, which are tied up in the stories we tell ourselves about ourselves.

We explode into this world with a lot of "stuff" in our DNA. Our genes, our transgenerational "baggage," the reality that we may feel some kinda way about things right out of the gate. These are all a big part of the truth puzzle. What we do with this stuff is up to us. And fearing it gets us nowhere.

Let me tell you a story about two guys who one night came up against their identities and the fear of facing them.

Around 2012, during my "second wave" of standup, a bunch of fellow comedian friends and I were finishing a show at the HaHa in North Hollywood and decided to venture deep into the San Fernando Valley to catch a late-night open mic. The sprawling sports bar was packed, even at 1 a.m., and the sign-up list wasn't even that long. Good intel! We signed up and hit the bar.

The makeshift stage was a mic stand in the dead center of the room. Comedy in the round. Awesome! The young comic onstage wasn't doing particularly well, but that's what open mics are for. He was getting heckled. Good for him!

As we surveyed the crowd, we noticed the heckling was coming from a couple of skinheads. Being Jewish, my eye can usually pick up a swastika in the room. The first one I noticed was on a small and wiry guy—it was easy to spot because it was on his face. Upon broader inspection, there was a lot of leather and chain link amidst this sea of rowdy patrons, several others also sported similar skinhead artwork.

For our part, we were a diverse group of comedians to begin with, but only now did we appreciate how different we were from most of the crowd. The neo-heckler with the prominent swastika was especially drunk. I think most of us were pretty buzzed, but he was crossing over, going a little dark, cursing at the comic, who ended his set and left the stage. Someone in our group suggested we leave before one of our names was called. Just then, I heard "HERSH!"

Having a name like Hersh is akin to wearing the Jewish skull cap, known as the "yarmulka." The heckler's eyes opened wide, and he smiled wickedly. I had that feeling you get when staring at a rabid, vicious dog: if I run, it will smell fear and attack. Bar shows are tough to begin with. People are not necessarily there for the comedy, so they are loud in the best of circumstances.

I had a decent amount of material at that juncture, and I could have done a universal bit about drinking or something, and I'm pretty sure no one would have even heard it. I could have opted for my signature "Scarface as a Comedian" bit, but that had nothing to do with the energy in the room, which was weird. I definitely got the sense that little wild-eyes was on the prowl, so going low key was not the play. And as I mentioned, this bar was big and packed. A collective response was called for.

I made a decision. I chose a bit that had been hit and miss but felt right for the moment. I took the mic and held up three fingers, calling on my resonant voice to make sure the whole room heard me. "THERE ARE THREE RULES OF ISRAELI COMEDY!" I shouted in an unmistakable foreign accent. The room settled down. Neo-heckler looked at his buddy in disbelief. His pal, big and more docile than his friend, cocked his head.

"RULE NUMBER ONE: IT'S SHUT THE F%&* UP TIME!"

I think I heard laughter. I don't know what I saw because I wasn't making eye contact. Yet.

"RULE NUMBER TWO: SAME AS RULE NUMBER ONE. BUT IF YOU NOT SHUTTING THE F%&* UP, IT'S GONNA BE PROBLEM. I GIVE YOU A SOCIAL MEDIA ANALOGY..." I said, making my accent even thicker.

This is where I looked wiry neo-heckler-nazi in the eyes. There was only air between him at the bar, and me, maybe a couple yards away at the mic.

"IF YOU NOT GONNA STAY OUT OF MYSPACE, I'M GONNA F%&* UP YOUR FACEBOOK!" I lifted my eyes up to the big buddy and smiled.

"What's Rule #3?" mini-nazi shouted.

To my fellow comics' credit, none of them had left by this point. "LEMME TELL YOU, JACK—YOU DON'T EVEN WANNA *HEAR* RULE #3!"

Wiry, drunk, neo-nazi-heckler burst out laughing and strode right up to me, throwing his arm around my shoulder, handing me his beer. "I love this guy!" he exclaimed.

I took the beer and nodded my thanks, taking a sip.

It was a surreal moment, and I knew this was the best we were gonna get. The next comic was called up. It was probably one of our group, but we'd just won the survival lottery, and we were not gonna hang around to feed the slots. Big bear skinhead called his little friend back to the bar, and I rejoined my buddies, exiting in a jovial mood as we might after any good set.

In retrospect, a few things worked in my favor: First, my small size ran counter to the imposing character I was playing, creating a comedic visual paradox. Second, the bigger dude and I connected in that one moment when I smiled at him, both of us knowing we were managing his powder keg of a drunk friend. And lastly, I addressed the tension, but not at the expense of the neo-wiener schnitzel. I was bold enough to *go up*, earning some points in the room.

But what I think really happened is that a couple of guys with seemingly conflicting identities, who could have caved to fear tactics, instead brushed up against one another and directed an alternative outcome. See, I don't know why mini-nazi had a swastika on his face. I don't know what his chunk of DNA contains. In fact, for all I know this kid was Jewish (I've known people born into the Jewish faith who resent the enmity often directed at them and thus adopt an antisemitic position as something of a survival mechanism). What I think happened in that bar was that I was bold in making a joke out of the very idea of "toughness" and "macho," and ass-kicking in general. And I did not do it at anyone's expense. So, while I don't know the inner story of mini-nazi, I know mine. And I gave the two of us an out, based on what we had in common: that little guys act tough to survive, and we look silly doing it. There was no lying in that moment. We decided fearlessly to *like* ourselves, and even each other... for a moment.

"I DON'T CARE WHAT ANYBODY THINKS!"

Finally, if we are going to be totally truthful with ourselves, we have to get real about this little gem, which I hear more often than I care to. Whaaa...? I find myself thinking when it gets thrown around. Are you immortal? A higher life form, separate and apart from the homosapien collective? Of course, we all care what people think of us, if we're going to be quite honest with ourselves. Sometimes it's intended as a compliment, or an aspiration, even. But there is quite a bit of road between self-confidence, a unique point of view, relative independence, and literally not caring for the opinions of others.

With introspection comes knowledge of oneself, and with this knowledge comes the ability to seek the wise counsel of others. A true leader should care and want to know what people think. They seek out those with more detailed knowledge of a subject, close confidants with deeper expertise, and specific qualities that complement and support their own leadership (we will discuss this more in *Chapter 4* on the importance of third-party validation).

Who are these confidants for you? What have they learned that you wish to understand? Is there balance in their life, and if so, how was it achieved? Are you making the most of these relationships? Do they perceive truths about you that you are resisting?

Once you open the door to this honest self-discovery, you'll be amazed by the resources at your disposal.

And it isn't about "what other people think." It's about "what people who care about you think" and the truths you have uncovered within yourself.

You can't know or find yourself until you are completely honest with yourself. Fess up! Get real, even when it's uncomfortable or embarrassing, and especially when it's scary (I can still smell that bar in the San Fernando Valley!). Fear of being vulnerable about your own truths is one of the biggest roadblocks to helping those you lead, influence, and work with to sell the truth. So, if you're keeping some truths from yourself, some lessons you need to learn, exploration opens the door to self-honesty, which allows you to question your identity, your purpose, and your brand.

Confronting reality is *the* gateway to selling the truth and one you'll need to be comfortable with when we move on to the next chapter, where we will talk about how to confront the Spin Doctors and Bullshit Artists who impede our best efforts to sell the truth.

MONSEIGNEUR CLAUDE FROLLO
The Hunchback of Notre Dame

Out of the ashes of the Black Plague, Dom Claude Frollo rose through his studies to become the Archdeacon of Josas. He and his brother were orphaned when their parents succumbed, and so, putting "family first," Frollo tended to his alcoholic brother, funding his care by playing a small flute.

Frollo also served as rescuer to a deformed, abandoned, hunchback child, whom he adopted and raised as his son, teaching young "Quasimodo" a kind of sign language in the wake of deafness caused by the cathedral bells.

A revered scholar, whose knowledge spans language, law, medicine, science, and of course, theology, Frollo also explores alternative medicine, very forward-thinking for his time. He does this despite the judgments of the wider community, placing his mission above scorn and scandal. He does the same in his interactions with Esmeralda, a gypsy girl with inappropriate designs on a Captain Phoebus de Chateaupers. Frollo risks all to intervene, but alas not all souls can be saved. Sometimes, the passions of mere mortals lead to their undoing, despite the best efforts of those purer of soul. Some do-gooders are punished by fate, and yet, the telling of their stories defies the ravages of time.

✧

Hypocrisy, in and of itself, seems to me like something of an inevitability. It irks me when one person tells another, "You're a hypocrite!" Of course, you are! We are all constantly engaged in a process of trial and error. We get things wrong. We set out to do one thing, and the result is something different. We hope to behave one way but don't live up to our expectations. What matters is how we handle it.

Now, pious hypocrisy like Frollo's? That doesn't wash with me. It shouldn't undo any good we've done outside of our failings. But it doesn't wash. The original *Hunchback of Notre Dame* story, written by Victor Hugo and published in 1831, has yielded what is arguably the most despicable Disney villain—the murderous, lustful, and abusive, Claude Frollo. And if we were to take the bio exercise even further, we might conclude that Frollo was way too hard on himself. The positive lesson to extract from his experience might be that idealization sounds a lot like idolization. And we would do well to steer clear of both.

Our buddy Frollo isn't trying to be good. He is appropriating the concept of piety and spinning it to his advantage. He knows the pitfalls of human nature and the power of fear (as well as the fear of power). He is not at war with his desires. Rather, he is a seducer of the vulnerable, so driven by his own darkness that he is a shameless hypocrite, selling that in which he does not believe. He is the worst kind of Bullshit Artist because he is cloaked in the sacred whilst desecrating it.

CHAPTER 4

THE SPIN DOCTOR, THE BULLSHIT ARTIST, AND OTHER SEDUCERS WE DON'T WANT TO KNOW, LIKE, OR TRUST

O ver the last few chapters, I have attempted to help you see how difficult we sometimes find it to fathom our own ridiculousness—how we often engage in a continuous cover-up of our own vulnerability. As I mentioned in the Introduction, so terrified are we these days of our own minds that we've willingly replaced them with fake realities, some of our making, and some pushed on us by others. The last three chapters have been about exposing all that BS so we can better build our own personal brand. By facing who we really are, finding what we really value and cherish, and then being brave enough not to lie about it all to ourselves, we can help others discover their own values and how to be true to their own brands, products, teams, and organizations.

In this chapter, we will look at how hard it can be to fathom the ridiculousness of others, and the importance of not being seduced by the glitter of spin doctoring, bullshit artistry, and other popular marketing devices used in place of the actual truth in our branding and leadership. It's important to appreciate *how* we communicate—whether with honesty and integrity, or caving to the easier way of letting the compulsive liars tell our stories, brand our products, and lead our companies.

My take is this: for all the lip service paid to "Gen Z" and its hunger for "authenticity," what's really happened is that we've maxed out on nonsense and distraction (what I call "fauxthenticity") to the point where, as a society, we are *dizzy*. A line in Barry Levinson's 1982 film, *Diner*—where Tim Daly's character tells a drunk cellmate, "I'll hit you so hard, I'll kill your whole family"—pretty much sums up how much the current generation has inherited the punches we've taken over the past hundred years when it comes to all this spin doctoring and bullshitting. We've been so smacked around by it that we are literally punch drunk.

It's time to sober up.

As a brand marketer or business leader, you can either go for the knockout and rifle through the pockets of the sprawled-out consumer, or you can check yourself, steady your own hand on the shoulder of your neighbor—your customer, team, constituents—look them in the eye, and *sell the truth*.

What's it going to be?

I'm tackling this stuff now in the book because to embrace the truth we must decide not to tolerate lying in any form—whether it's a translucent lie we tell ourselves (revisit *Chapter 3*), or something bigger and often more insidious in the form of BS-ing others.

KNOWING NO. 4: DON'T BE SEDUCED BY THE SIREN SONG OF WILLFUL DECEIVERS

This Knowing means that no matter how commonplace deception has become, we have to work harder to combat and reject it. Although conscious, willful deception cannot be stopped, and such deceivers can't stop themselves even if they wanted to (so accustomed they have become to lying, about everything), we must avoid being swept up by them.— There is no shortcut to the results you want, so you're gonna have to work with the truth, steering clear of that insidious sound such deceivers make, turning the boat back home where Penelope keeps the fires of fidelity burning.

Seduction, by the way, is the lure of satisfaction. —It's a tease and is easiest to spot when the suggestion of gratification begins to wind its way into our brain.

But consider any encounters you may have had with seduction: was getting satisfaction the end result? Really? The word "seduction" is most often associated with sex and money, but for simplicity's sake, let's look at the context of conflict. Let's say you are seduced by a leader or movement that speaks to your feelings of disaffection, dismissal, oppression, and so forth. This stirs up resentment—even hatred—within you, and with the encouragement of your "people," you engage in a full conflict where you compromise the values you supposedly hold dear and rationalize your dismissal of said values. In the end, those people you don't like get hurt, possibly wiped out, and your agenda is fulfilled. Now the world looks very different. Are you happy? Are you satisfied? What did all the conflict get you? What did your bitterness, resentment, and hatred buy you? Instead of judging seduction by its values in the moment, consider the outcome. Is this the outcome you want?

Conversely, imagine the sting of the truth—the unpopularity, perhaps, of that position—the inconvenience of not getting immediate gratification or the contentment of letting off steam. Should you remain vigilant and resistant to the siren songs, strong in your beliefs, what does the outcome look like now? Is this the outcome you want?

This is the process in which I engage when I work with a client. Before we can become partners in the telling of their story, we deeply examine the possible outcomes. Since everything we say must be true (for me, there's no flexibility around that point), we must get to a place where we are happy about the truth, where we see the benefits of it and how it serves our audience.

The Spin Doctors and Bullshit Artists I have encountered, on the other hand, are not the least bit interested in selling the truth. Rather, they are intent on weakening and cheapening the truth by telling us what we want to hear, by seducing us with the pull of getting immediate satisfaction. In some way, theirs is a "solution" to our "problem," which is precisely why we are prone to accept their statements as fact. Plus, it takes a lot of energy to shoot down falsehoods, and our failure to do so can be interpreted or used as tacit approval. So, the lie begins to gain traction.

As a lover of language, I appreciate the ways in which words can be manipulated for impact. But I contend that it's laziness or ineptitude that keeps business leaders and brand managers from dealing honestly and openly in their communication, leaving it to the Bullshit Artists and Spin Doctors instead, letting them twist and manipulate the messages into a song that is hard to resist and oh so easy to listen to.

SHORTCUT TO A DITCH

To understand further how to avoid compulsive deceivers, we must truly understand *spinning*.

To spin is lead your audience (customers/associates/team/ business) away from the truth. It's a natural tendency that begins in childhood. We don't want to disappoint our parents or get in trouble, so we "spin" the story away from our own culpability: "I went outside to make sure none of the other kids were doing anything bad…" This continues in our teenage years. "She said she couldn't do it, so I just did it, so you wouldn't have to." ("She" is the moniker Mom takes on between the ages of 13 and 17.)

The "Spin Doctor," while ingrained in our consciousness as a clever and useful team member, has no place in branding and business. It's a crisis management role, and even then, I reject it for a number of reasons:

- Spinning presumes the gullibility of the audience, so the risk of making things worse is immediate.
- Disinformation is a band-aid at best, and eventually it will be ripped off—by you, or someone else.
- The truth is more powerful when you own it.
- If there's a problem, pretending it isn't there will not make it go away.
- As Mark Twain said, "If you tell the truth you don't have to remember anything."

Compared to the Spin Doctor, the Bullshit Artist is less useful still. A spin doctor may at least have the good intention of sparing their client embarrassment over a regrettable incident. The Bullshit Artist is typically engaged in self-preservation and is weaving a litany of lies so disconnected from the truth that the only eventual outcome is total image immolation. Where a Spin Doctor might change strategies, a Bullshit Artist commits to wherever the narrative takes them. This leads to their storytelling wearing thin, due to the randomness, intricacy, and desperation of their lies.

For example, imagine you have hired Lemil to watch your beloved cat while you go on vacation, and upon your return, the cat, Miss Evelyne, is nowhere to be found. Lemil appears as baffled as you are:

Lemil: I don't understand.

You: What don't you understand? Where is Miss Evelyne?

Lemil: *Where* is she? (*walking around the house*) Evelyne! Miss Evelyne! She was here a minute ago. The front door. Did you leave the front door open?

You: She doesn't run out the front door!

Lemil: Obviously, she's here, then. I didn't lose your cat, for Pete's sake (*laughs*). I mean nobody takes care of a cat like I do. Look, here's her yarn—she did the funniest trick with her yarn today.

You: (*looking around the kitchen*) What's this? This is veal! And it's for dogs! Miss Evelyne doesn't eat meat!

Lemil: Of course, she doesn't eat meat. I know that. The store delivered it by mistake. I opened it before I realized it was the wrong item...

You: There are two full scoops missing! You fed her this poison!

Lemil: Absolutely not! Oh my God! How could you think that?

The Bullshit Artist pushes credulity to the limit. They're also likable enough and so committed to the lie that you want to believe them.

Lemil: Let's run upstairs. Miss Evelyne is probably on your bed...but honestly, I'm kind of pissed off that you would jump to the conclusion that I *(heading upstairs)* ... Evelyne! Miss Evelyne! Where are you, sweetheart?

Indignance is another telltale sign of Bullshit Artistry.

You: Ahhhhh!

Lemil: What?

You: There's a fresh mound of dirt in the yard! You killed her and buried her there!

Lemil: *Buried* her? Now, you're just messing with me. Is that it? You're messing with me. It's not funny, considering I did you a huge favor staying here for four days.

Bullshit Artists are also notable for their lack of shame. And it's worth mentioning that those who tend to be vulnerable to this crap are projecting a deep want onto the bullshitter. They really want the B.A. to be reliable, trustworthy, and whatever else they subconsciously know them *not* to be. So, on the other side of the B.A. is someone who hasn't learned the Knowing from Chapter 3.

You: So, if I go outside and dig up that mound of dirt, there's no way I'm going to find Miss Evelyne in there?

Lemil: Absolutely not!

(You grab a shovel and race out back.)

Lemil: And even if you did find her in there, I'm pretty sure she was alive when she got in there. Like a joke gone wrong. You know what a joker she is. I really hope to God she did not get in there thinking it was going to be funny.

You: (discovering something under the dirt) *Aaaaaaaaaaaaaaaahhhhhhhh!*

Lemil: Dammit, she did, didn't she? Let's hope she's okay.

Do Bullshit Artists enjoy a good long run sometimes? Sure. Can they benefit from this book? Of course! This book is about growing, as well as moving through the challenges of brand building and business leadership (but you and I both know, Bullshit Artists don't necessarily want to grow). The truth is...

- The truth just doesn't appeal to them all that much.
- The "compulsive liar" is a thing. They would sooner lie than tell the truth. And while this may be subconscious (or semi-conscious), they may well be addicted to lying.
- It isn't always malicious, but it is very insidious. You could really even like the person (so appealing, sometimes, like a Siren), but the message is still hurtful and harmful, even if they haven't meant it to be.

We don't need anyone to sugarcoat the truth for us (which is often what Bullshit Artists and Spin Doctors are all about). In the larger sense, I'd say that for human beings to expect only good news and good times is so unrealistic as to be harmful. Just as we really don't want our kids to feel pain, disappointment, sadness, and depression, these are part of life. So, if we shield them from these things, we're setting them up for a rude awakening under less sympathetic circumstances. The truth often hurts, but only for a minute. Misinformation, half-truths, outright lies, and patronizing tales peddled by Spin Doctors and Bullshit Artists are actually the hardest to swallow.

THE ENEMY WITHIN

"Okay," you're saying, "so we must be on the lookout for Spin Doctors and Bullshit Artists. And we should recognize the telltale signs. We get it. Let's move on to the next Know..."

Not so fast...

We need to go a little deeper. When we have less faith in humanity, we may actually be *more* vulnerable to Bullshit because we want so desperately to connect with people and ideas in which we can believe. In the post-COVID world, for example, entrepreneurs, small business owners, coaches, and consultants have thrived online in mastermind classes, networking groups, webinars, and via social media messaging. This has become a popular strategy for growing one's contact and customer base. But with all that, the fact is, some of the BS artists use all this social media, technology, and faceless online marketing to their advantage, grinding it out so hard you gotta wonder why they don't just create a great product to sell.

I almost got taken by one such grinder a year or so ago. This BS-er had applied to appear on one of my podcasts, and I hit it off with him (or so I thought), and when he pitched an event, I bit. His program was basically stolen from another coach (as a result, some of it was useful, but the event was a paid upsell to a larger program and some fell for it). I met some amazing people who likewise attended this event, however, and I consider my money well-spent for that reason. This wasn't a swindle, per se; it was a stolen, semi-useful program that relied on the seduction of vulnerable people hungry to connect with others whom they wanted so badly to believe in, using what each wished were true about the other.

Fortunately, this all happened to me *before* I published that particular podcast episode, so I avoided sharing this spin doctor's BS story with my audience. It was a great story, mind you, but it was 50 percent Bullshit. And that 50 percent is the part that you'd end up paying through the nose for if you hired such a person.

I do want to mention here, as an important aside, a final warning on the subject of conscious deceivers. Sometimes the most dangerous of all such deceptive "snakes" are slithering even deeper in the grass than the Spin Doctors and Bullshit Artists. Such snakes, which I'm only going to mention briefly, are what I call Con Artists. These types are Bullshit Artists with malicious intent, and instead of peddling a story that is only 50 percent true, theirs is closer to 97 percent bull crap. The carrot they dangle isn't money, nor are they asking for money at first—they dangle relief in front of you, a solution to your problem. And if you don't actually have the problem, they will create it for you. "Con" stands for confidence. They are artists who weave a web of faith into which you will become entrapped, and they have no regard for the harm done to you. It is, quite plainly, their nature. Most politicians, for example, are not scorpions because they're politicians. They are politicians because they are scorpions. Take care around such people.

For a real-world example of such a Con Artist, let me tell you briefly about a Siren I'll call Blake Heavenly. Blake reached out to me on LinkedIn, cold but with 10 connections in common. He purported to be a life and executive business coach, and in our brief meet-and-greet over Zoom, shared some impressive insights into my life and business. All pretty typical these days. I made it clear I was not in a position to acquire coaching services, which Blake said was fine. He did feel we were aligned in terms of our complementary offerings. He said he was putting together a live event in a few months and asked if I'd like to participate in some way. It seemed like a great opportunity to do more speaking engagements in the ramp up to my book release. Blake presented as a baby-faced, G-d-fearing widower with a gift for cutting to the essential purpose of a person, as well as a keen business sense. He looked and sounded the part.

When we met again over Zoom to discuss the details, Blake was calling from a loud coffee shop, which was very 2005, something that was repeated in every subsequent conversation. Alternately, Blake would appear on Zoom from somewhere quieter but with the same blurred background, which was the back of a van. He said this was his mobile home, a lifestyle he pursued after the passing of his late wife. of whom he spoke often at first, though I don't recall him saying her name more than once, if that.

The real warning signs appeared when we set about crafting a one-sheet about the event: Blake was very comfortable swiping copy from a successful event done by someone else and adapting it. His explanation: "I've studied the marketing and combined the best elements to optimize effectiveness." Since it was a temporary document that wasn't going live, I acquiesced, crafting original sections to replace the swiped copy. So, at that point, I was writing the copy, but what Blake had done was, well, nothing but move existing puzzle pieces around.

I asked Blake to add testimonials, which he did, using only the first names of his clients. "A testimonial from Emanuel Z. is fine for a skincare product," I told him, "But not for a coach." Blake said he would reach out to the clients for permission to use their full names. In the meantime, I realized this dude's LinkedIn did not really include a bio, so much as a statement about his coaching practice. His Facebook featured masterclass-style videotaped talks, with no audience. I then checked with two of our shared contacts on

LinkedIn: both good friends of mine, but neither could recall how or when they'd connected with Blake.

Okay, I'm pretty sure this is not gonna happen, I thought to myself.

We were awaiting confirmation of the venue (which had purportedly been locked in), when Blake called about a business he'd operated "since I was 16," and from which he derived the bulk of his income. It was a loan business that seemed shady, and further, he suggested I run a quick credit check using a safe service he recommended (a legit identity protection service), sharing the login with him(!). I asked him to send an email with all the details of the proposed business opportunity.

"Okay! Great!" he replied.

The email never came.

I took a look at his website, which used stock footage, and when I heard a voiceover *in his voice* speaking about him in the third person, the lack of legitimacy was complete.

He texted that afternoon with great news: a client of his had signed up for the event!

"Awesome, who is it?" I texted back.

"Let me collect the payment first lol!" he responded.

Uh-huh.

I explained to him that for all his insights into the human condition and his understanding of many aspects of business, he was unable to provide the third-party validation needed to successfully market this event. I made it about the lack of credibility his audience would perceive, but the message was clear: I'm onto you, and I'm out.

The loan scam aside, the event itself would not have been a big moneymaker. The lure was the chance to give a couple of talks about *Selling the Truth* and knowing oneself while capturing broadcast quality audio and video, along with some awesome video testimonials. Blake and I were after the same thing: validation. The difference between us was that I was brimming with truth, and Blake was nothing more than a Con Artist full of shit.

KNOW-LIKE-TRUST

This chapter has been about more than fraud prevention. At this point in my life, I should have drawn a conclusion about Blake much earlier in the process. But I let my enthusiasm and sense of momentum take precedence over a very simple principle: If you want to apply Knowing No. 4 and avoid the seduction of conscious deceivers, you've got to establish "Know-Like-Trust." There's a reason "Know" comes first. Once you know yourself, your job is to know who you're dealing with.

The "Like" part has to do with not becoming smitten, no matter how easy it is to be drawn to others. As I've shared previously, we may really like some people right out of the gate, but that doesn't mean we should, without doing some due diligence. I can use myself as a case in point. The same qualities that make me a great "truth seller" and an empathetic Message Therapist have left me vulnerable to the Like. I know myself—I have to be careful on this one. Be sure you know whether this is one of your vulnerabilities as well.

The "Trust" part is built over time, so it takes the longest to establish. All three are integral to selling the truth, and in the next chapter, we'll get into more about the Know-Like-Trust guideline in terms of reputation-building and how third-party validation plays into all of that.

THANOS
Avengers, Guardians of the Galaxy

It takes a good deal of determination and grit to bring stability to the universe. It is also a thankless task that is not so much accomplished as relentlessly pursued. Some would say it requires superhuman strength. Amazingly, Thanos fits this bill. Born to A'Lars of the Titans, Thanos set a fine example of unconditional love for his people and desperately sought to save them from starvation, though some lacked the sophistication to appreciate his remedies. As a result of Thanos' ideas being rejected, planet Titan was devastated, leaving Thanos the sole survivor and forcing him to seek meaning outside of his comfort zone. He found his calling as a gemologist of sorts, and his quest for the six "Infinity Stones" is the stuff of legend.

Beyond the brawn (he stands 6 feet, 7 inches and comports himself with unusual grace given his reported 985 pounds), Thanos is a surrogate father to the "Children of Thanos," six kids he adopted while visiting their respective planets of origin. Tragically, much of the population of the children's planets were wiped out, and had Thanos not been present at those exact moments, his wards would no doubt have perished along with their people.

Thanos' accomplishments reveal an appreciation for the importance of collaboration and include the Infinity Gauntlet, a glove designed to channel the power of the six Infinity Stones. He enlisted the help of the Dwarf King, Eitri, and his fellow dwarves to craft the gauntlet, demonstrating that big or small, each of us brings something important to the table. Eitri retired from craftsmanship shortly thereafter, as it was unlikely he would ever again match the standard of artisanal excellence he achieved while working with Thanos. Thanos continues to crusade for the preservation of natural resources. Though he can envision a peaceful conclusion to his adventures ("I finally rest and watch the sunrise on a grateful universe," he once told his acquaintance, Dr. Stephen Vincent Strange), he has no immediate plans to retire. "The hardest choices," he observes, "require the strongest wills."

✍

My first supervillain Legit Bio is for a character who sees his actions as justified. Created by writer-artist Jim Starlin, Thanos first appeared in *The Invincible Iron Man #55* (cover date February 1973). In the Marvel films, Thanos is played by Josh Brolin, who brings the complexity of the character to his performance. My intention in crafting this bio is to show how branding isn't all about self-image. It is tied to perception, to third-party validation, if you will, and the "stuff of legend" relies heavily on that validating voice of the storyteller.

CHAPTER 5

THIRD PARTY VALIDATION AND WHY YOU SHOULD LISTEN TO HERSH

L et's start this out with a shout out to sidekicks. Isn't it ironic that The Lone Ranger was never seen without Tonto by his side? One published theory is that, after 11 episodes of the TV series, the producers decided LR needed someone to talk to. But I have a different idea: Though the Ranger stands alone, he needs third-party validation, a sidekick, an advance man, so when he rides into a new town and people say, "Who is that masked man?" Tonto can explain, without revealing LR's name of course.

What are we talking about here, with this third-party validation, and who needs it? Are the Lone Ranger, Batman, and other superheroes the only darlings worthy of such endorsement? Why is it important in our efforts to sell the truth? In this chapter, we'll take a closer look at why it matters and how it really works.

Third-party validation comes through word of mouth, "grassroots marketing," seeding, events, networking, testimonials, referrals, guesting on podcasts, and "influencers." Any of these can be integral to your efforts to get real and stay real.

Let's say you're at a party—meeting someone new, and you want to *sell the truth* about yourself—the last thing you want to talk about is yourself. The ideal situation, if asked, is to give a very general, modest reference to your vocation i.e., "I sell shoes," as opposed to "I own a chain of shoe stores." Next, ask about the other person, sincerely trying to understand their role and perspective. Thankfully, within a moment or two, a third party arrives, perhaps someone who knows you both, and instinctively begins singing both of your praises. This is a game-changer. Credibility is key, of course. There's no validation without verification. And what's beautiful about third-party validation is it inspires us to live up to the hype. It keeps us on our toes, spurs us to be our best. That's the fun part, in my humble opinion, making the people who referred us look good. They teed us up; we smashed it, and now they look great for having recommended us. They now receive credible third-party validation from us. There's nothing like this circular endorsement for getting the best out of ourselves and others, nothing like giving our clients, teams, organizations, and customers confidence in our devotion to telling the truth. After all, we don't want to make them look like a liar, now do we?

LAY DOWN YOUR POM POMS

"But Hersh," you may be thinking, "isn't this just so much hype?" No, third-party validation is not cheerleading; it is much more grounded in quiet confidence than that. Cheerleading is overt, and when we are networking, we can definitely do without the pom poms. Besides, cheerleading is to boost the confidence of the player, not to convince the audience that the player is strong. "You got this, Stephanie!" That may inspire Stephanie to make the free throw, but it doesn't make me wanna buy from her. That said, third-party validation *is* a great confidence booster. This is because your colleague is putting their reputation on the line in speaking highly of you. So, there's no reason to doubt their sincerity.

The knowing here isn't just to "have people say nice things about you." It's more of an approach to life and business—the idea that how you treat people matters. Thoughtfulness matters. Sure, some of what we do is strategic, but it's more often the "accidental relationships," and "incidental courtesies" that prove most pivotal, especially if you want your reputation to precede you.

KNOWING NO. 5: YOU DON'T HAVE TO SELL YOUR TRUTH IF OTHERS SELL IT FOR YOU

Third-party validators with whom you have relationships are more than willing to tell others about that relationship and how you have treated it. You've already laid the groundwork with these validators, so they know that you can be trusted and now that trust can be transferred. In a way, it's almost like a transfer of energy where the third-party validator can tip off others about your integrity, credibility, and character. Basically, they are selling you, so you don't have to sell yourself, and that's infinitely more powerful when it comes to brand building, leadership, and improving company culture than trying to convince others that you're all that.

MENTORS (AKA THIRD-PARTY VALIDATORS) AND LITTLE KID SYNDROME

Okay, so how old do you feel? I ask this of all readers, regardless of age, because I don't think it matters how old you are; you either feel like an adult or you feel like a kid.

At 57, I am finally on the verge of conquering a chronic condition I call "Little Kid Syndrome."

Little Kid Syndrome: The sensation of being the "little kid" in conversations with adults, particularly authority figures. This condition is not immaturity or even marked by immaturity; it's simply a failure to assume the "authoritative grown-up posture," regardless of age and status.

Perhaps being the youngest of three siblings (and constantly referred to as "the baby" of the family) has something to do with it. When I am approached by a police officer, for instance, I feel like the child in that exchange, or at least the junior player, regardless of their age. At parent-teacher conferences, I have a similar disposition. Handymen, plumbers, accountants, and attorneys have the same effect. In short, I have felt, for a good portion of my life, like the little kid around people who I believe know something I don't.

Thankfully, this does not happen with clients. Why? Because they are eliciting my help, and in this area, regardless of age, I am the expert. I am their third-party validator. I know my power.

It may be subtle. But when I asked if you feel like an adult or a kid, you had an internal reaction—you're either the authority figure yourself, or a citizen.

Can someone with Little Kid Syndrome be a leader, a third-party validator, a mentor? Apparently, yes. I've led companies, film and stage productions, media campaigns, and more. Now, am I a "thought leader?" To quote Nigel Tufnel (Christopher Guest) in *This is Spinal Tap*, "I don't know. What are the hours?" The truth is that's a third-party question.

I do know that a leader is willing to learn. The willingness to absorb lessons, the hunger to learn, that basic humility, certainly carries enormous benefits in the realization of our potential. So, in that sense, Little Kid Syndrome is an advantage.

But somewhere between humility and self-confidence is the sweet spot. As we move through this book together—whichever pole we're working from—it is my hope that we'll each hit that mark in our approach to life and business. That we'll see that how we treat others (and allow others to treat us) matters. That no matter where we are in our personal life or in our business and leadership endeavors, we will come to understand that beyond the strategy, our relationships with others and the incidental courtesies we afford each other are the most pivotal.

Case in point, everything good that has happened to me in the past few years can be traced in some way to these pivotal relationships. I approached them with humility, and they rewarded me with life lessons, business lessons, and third-party credibility. The people I formed these invaluable relationships with became my mentors and have shaped my career in ways I could never have fathomed when I first crossed paths with them.

CARL FORSBERG AND BRIAN SHUSTER

My first professional mentors have mostly me in common, and I don't think they've ever met. But they were hugely influential around the same time, my early 20s, when I had just completed my undergraduate education (at Yeshiva University) and some post-graduate study at the School of Visual Arts (SVA).

I was living in New York, hoping to make it as a screenwriter, but working as a "junior rep," essentially an assistant to the representative for directors, composers, and sound designers who work on commercials. Through my SVA professors, I'd spent the summer as a production assistant on a low budget movie. I'd also been encouraged by the chairman of SVA, George McGuinness, to study advertising, because as he put it, "You could sell a line on a piece of paper." I did not love that assessment because I believed I was a "creative," the opposite of a "salesman." Of course, in advertising, creatives *are* salespeople, but I didn't really want to accept that at the time. At George's urging, however, I took a course in commercial production. That led to a gig with Carl Forsberg, the East Coast Sales Rep for a commercial production company called Luna Pier Films.

CARL

The first time Carl and I met was over lunch, and one of the first things he said to me was, "You remind me of a young Robert Downey, Jr." This was funny because Downey is only seven months older than I am. But you see? Little Kid Syndrome. I think it extends to other people's perceptions of us as well, not just our own. I suspect Carl carries some of that Little Kid Syndrome himself, which is why we get along so well to this day, and why the boss-employee dynamic felt somewhat atypical.

When Carl and I first started working together, I was kind of like a Russian doll with a yarmulke—fresh out of Yeshiva College and SVA, Sabbath observant, strictly kosher, and seeking success as a screenwriter (because acting and standup comedy meant working on Shabbos). Carl, on the other hand, was raised Lutheran in Westfield,

New Jersey, to a cancer surgeon dad and a stay-at-home mom, spent summers as a caddy at the country club, and is someone whose life experience was about as different from mine as could be. He has charm to spare and is unfailingly decent. He cleans up nice but does not shy away from his mistakes and does not pretend to know it all. He did well as a salesman because he tried to be a resource. "Be a resource" is one of the most valuable lessons I learned from him. He did his best to position me for success and was supportive of my Hollywood goals.

Eventually, Carl and I got into a really good groove. My main function for him was creating bios, press releases, and blurbs about the latest work and talent, arming him with meaty, third-party validation of the artists he was pitching. While I hated cold-calling agency producers and pitching business, I loved writing bios that made it easier for reps like Carl to pitch these artists. Since I was about to get married, and my fiancé was starting law school, I needed to make money. Carl was single, but let's just say he was engaged to the Treasury Department at the time. So, we each wanted the other to do well. Our work together became symbiotic, circular. He made me look good, and I did my best to help his business be successful. The incidental courtesies we afforded each other proved to be significant. He thrived as a sales rep, and I shined as a publicist for the commercial production and post business.

All told, I worked with Carl on and off for about eight years—through four production companies, and three children (mine). During my time with him, I represented luminary filmmakers like the Coen Brothers and Jodie Foster for commercials. I got to have lunch with Eric Clapton. I learned something about copywriting, developed my personality as a business professional, peeled away a couple of Russian doll layers, and discovered my knack for public relations. Through all this, Carl helped me gain credibility in an industry I didn't think I wanted to work in, supporting my creative endeavors and helping build my career.

In 1997 I moved to the West Coast to be closer to the film business, and Carl remained in New York. We reunited at times at industry events and for lunch here and there, but as I reached further into comedy, screenwriting, footwear marketing, and freelance copywriting, our paths crossed less and less. Whenever the opportunity arose to speak well of one another, we seized it, out of mutual affection and respect. And in 2021, after knowing each other for 32 years, our paths crossed again.

In the midst of COVID, business had slowed considerably. At exactly the right moment, Carl was representing a couple of production companies that needed PR, and he referred them to me. These were not one-offs, either. They were retainer situations, and they really helped me stay on my feet during a universally challenging time. The main thing to note is that Carl knew I was great at my job, and not only would I be a positive reflection on him (allowing him to "be a resource"), but the PR aided his sales efforts on the clients' behalf as well. Everybody won through this third-party validation because three decades earlier, we sold to one another the only thing we had back then—the truth about each other.

BRIAN

Concurrent with my early work with Carl, which eventually evolved me into a niche publicist, I was furiously writing screenplays, and I paid to have a couple of one-sheet synopses published in something called *The Hollywood Producers Story Directory*. These caught the eye of Brian Shuster, a young producer (I believe he and Carl are both about 10 years older than me, so he was about 33 at the time) with excellent taste and very good connections in Hollywood. Like Carl, Brian is warm and decent, but he has no traces of Little Kid Syndrome (Brian spent his teen years in Beverly Hills, where the play is to give the impression of control).

Brian taught me that in Hollywood, talent lays a great foundation, but its value is what the market will bear. In other words, talent isn't currency. Currency is currency. Relationships are currency. *Image* is currency. Leverage is also currency. And to be smart in Hollywood is to be respectful of and judicious with whichever currency you're using.

He hired me to rewrite the screenplay for a movie called *Can it Be Love* (aka *Spring Break Sorority Babes*), for which characters, locations, and schedules had already been set. It was my first screen credit. The second film Brian and I collaborated on was *Assault on Dome 4*, starring Bruce Campbell, and on which I had sole writing credit.

But the most fun we had together was developing my original screenplays. Brian is an extremely creative producer, and we spent many nights on the phone developing a handful of movies. They haven't been made, but I am extremely proud of them. My favorite is *Abduction,* a suspense film about a young girl who may be the reincarnation of a contract killer; her presence threatens the reputation of a high-profile industrialist, so the girl ends up on the run, under the protection of the courageous psychiatrist treating her. It came very close to getting made, and I hope someday it does. At the time, I saw my work as a publicist as separate and apart from my "creative" pursuits in film with Brian. But were they?

For a year or so, Carl and I worked for the leading television commercial production company, Harmony Pictures, in New York.

As a complete and utter coincidence, Brian's father was on the board of directors of Harmony Holdings in Los Angeles, which was a parent company to my employer. Random. But the universe is funny that way.

It certainly helped that our boss at Harmony, Jonathan Miller (another wonderful mentor, friend, and third-party validator), was aware of the connection; he was fully supportive of my screenwriting and even advocated for me with the board of directors when I proposed Harmony hire me as a contract screenwriter and publicist. "We're in the advertising business, not the movie business," I was told, so it didn't happen, but it was a signal that some of my career ambitions were destined to lay outside the traditional parameters. I made the same pitch to another production company I worked for when I moved to LA a few years later. Same response. I wanted there to be crossover, some way to make my show-biz talents jive with my publicist work experience, but when that didn't always happen, I was able to fall back on the third-party validation Brian gave me with this early advice: believe in yourself, follow your heart, and know your value in the marketplace, because those three things don't always align.

Brian's advice led me to this nugget that I offer to anyone with aspirations outside the traditional employer-employee dynamic: avoid parallel tracks. Don't pursue a dream job while advancing in a completely unrelated career. Align your endeavors so the dots are connected in some way. Remember, climbing two ladders at once is a great way to split your pants and land on your ass. This doesn't mean you shouldn't work at a pet shop during high school unless you want to be a veterinarian, but it does means when you get out into the real world of work, your *career* development should be aligned with your goals.

After garnering representation, writing and co-writing a dozen screenplays, racking up three feature film credits, and doing a hundred studio pitch meetings in Hollywood with my writing partner John Burns, my showbiz career still hadn't come together. I don't know if this is because I'd also been working in PR and advertising instead of devoting everything I had to filmmaking, or because I was so blinded by "blockbuster Hollywood" success that I missed some synergistic signpost merging the two.

Looking back, I think it had nothing to do with any of that. As I have noted in other chapters, I thought of myself as an open-minded individual raised within a closed-minded socio-religious construct that prevented me (in my mind) from really following the showbiz career path because it interfered with my family's expectations and religious beliefs. But the way things evolved, with the third-party validation I received from such mentors as Brian and Carl, I see now that the universe was trying to show me a bigger picture. I was actually closed-minded in ways I didn't realize. I was a gifted, imaginative, *honest* storyteller, and I was coming up in a world where great storytelling that could be used to sell the truth was desperately needed within the world of branding. Sure, I was a good actor, comedian, comedy writer, and screenwriter, but the kind of acting and standup I did at the time—character immersions that obscured the real me—should have been a tipoff that performance in those days was an escape act.

During that time of dishonesty with myself, it was a chore to explain my "job" to my parents, and it was a challenge for colleagues to provide proper third-party validation because I didn't know what I really wanted to be! This is exactly the problem I now endeavor to solve for clients through MESSAGE Therapy.

Years later, when I launched the *Truth Tastes Funny* podcast, IMDB had me make a choice: please, figure out who you wanna be! Today, Carl and Brian, whom I still admire, adore, and collaborate with, have gotten on board with how I have branded myself, and the way I can sell that truth, now that I finally know what it is. The first-party confusion I caused early in my career made third-party validation a challenge and a jumble. Like I said early on, "Before you brand yourself, know yourself." That will make the job of your fans so much easier.

"THEY HAVE ONE THING YOU HAVEN'T GOT: A TESTIMONIAL"

The third-party validation that grows organically over time through relationship-building is super important. At the same time, on a practical level, it is essential to show prospective customers proof of concept before they buy, which comes in the form of testimonials. Your clients want to know what to expect from an engagement with you. If you've done your job well, these should not be hard to get. The best time to ask for testimonials is after you've over delivered and before they've forgotten.

I think of it as collecting evidence and stockpiling proof of concept. Testimonials are not a workaround or substitute for good work—they are a validation of it. I stress this because when we do a job for someone, and they've paid us for our services, we may not expect a testimonial in return. After all, they're the client, and it's important to continue showing respect for them after the job is done. So, you do not need to get a testimonial from every client. But when you do ask for the testimonial flavor of third-party validation, here is some criteria for how to approach that request:

1. **Credibility is King**. This person is vouching for you, so your audience should either recognize them or be able to discern that this person is a big fish in their own pond.

2. **Exceptional is Better.** You want to get testimonials from people for whom you had the opportunity to go the extra mile. It may be your M.O. to overdeliver, but the standout performances will set you apart from the competition.

3. **Quality Before Quantity.** An assortment of satisfied customers is the goal, of course. But each testimonial should say something different about you, highlighting some core skill or advantage to working with you.

4. **Video is Best.** This provides an extra dose of validation because it will be longer than a quote and feel more like an endorsement than mere words in passing.

5. **Flustered is Good.** It's fine to feel a bit embarrassed by the superlative evaluation inherent in a great testimonial. If every word is true and comes from the heart, this is your chance to receive third-party validation in your best light.

If your testimonials meet these criteria, you can't go wrong.

To summarize, go out there and do your best to live the reputation you want to establish. Meanwhile, those who appreciate your efforts and good qualities will constitute your fan base. They will help verify your credibility; they will become your sidekick of sorts, and with that third-party validation accumulating, you won't have to feel uncomfortable reaching out for more formal endorsements. Remember that third-party validation is a two-way street. The common denominator is sincerity, which is after all, one of the best ways you can sell the truth. A mutual admiration society will always stand you in good stead, no matter where your journey takes you.

Now, sometimes, we must engage in the opposite of testimonial and third-party validation canvassing: damage control. When damage has been done, usually directness wins in these cases, and sometimes humor can be one of the most indirect (yet powerful) ways to be direct. In the next chapter, we will explore this important tool for dealing with the inevitable casualties we all suffer personally and professionally. Humor helps, not because we don't take our situations seriously but because it is the great equalizer. It diffuses tension. Comedy is our way of taking a shit on the elephant in the room.

On to that humor in Chapter 6!

HANNIBAL LECTER
The Silence of the Lambs

In modern scientific circles, there is an ongoing exploration of epigenetic imprinting—the notion that an adverse environment affects disease disposition and outcome beyond a single lifespan—the idea that we may inherit trauma going back generations.

We may never know what factors contributed to the makeup of the surgeon and psychiatrist turned forensic FBI consultant, Dr. Hannibal Lecter, considered brilliant by all accounts, certainly cultured, and an elevated conversationalist with a wicked wit. While his accomplishments as a psychiatrist tending to countless troubled patients may be attributable to some combination of genetics and personal fortitude, it is clear his achievements came despite—or perhaps because of—a highly specific life-shattering event. As a child in Lithuania in 1944, Hannibal witnessed an unthinkable horror: the murder and cannibalism of his sister Mischa, whom he'd adored, by a band of deserting Lithuanian POWs who had volunteered to fight for Germany. All that follows in his life must be measured against this moment, as must the lives saved by Hannibal through his consulting work with the FBI in support of their efforts to identify and capture serial killers.

When approached by the agency to help solve the baffling case of "Buffalo Bill," a terrifying and prolific serial killer of young women, Hannibal unravels the mystery that leads to the killer's demise, saving the life of Catherine Martin, who was to be his next victim. In the process, Hannibal forms a unique bond with Clarice Starling, the FBI trainee assigned to work with him, counseling the promising agent regarding her own traumatic history. Her star rises because of their collaboration, and their relationship remains one in which Hannibal is Clarice's protector, perhaps as a means of countering the darkness in both of their lives.

❧

Comedy is not the first word that comes to mind when you think of the 1991 Jonathan Demme film, *The Silence of the Lambs*, based on the 1988 psychological horror novel by Thomas Harris (which was a sequel to his 1981 novel, *Red Dragon*). There seems to be nothing funny in Anthony Hopkins' portrayal of Hannibal (a role for which Hopkins famously took home a Best Actor Oscar with only 16 minutes of screen time). But certainly, there is a very dark strain of humor that runs through the film. Each character has at least a few comments to trigger an uncomfortable chuckle or shudder, Lecter chief among them, especially with the last line of the movie: "I'm having an old friend for dinner." The "humor" of this line diffuses the tension of that concluding moment in the film, without diminishing the effectiveness of the storytelling: Lecter is referring to his nemesis, Dr. Chilton. He sees Chilton arriving in Borneo, and lets the audience know that he is literally going to eat the man that night. This makes us at once uncomfortable and titillated, particularly because Lecter is way more likable than Chilton, fiendish proclivities aside. In this case, humor is used to dilute horror.

Sometimes, when humor is used, it pushes the boundaries of good taste. Chapter 6 is about pushing boundaries as a brand, and how humor—though tricky—can accelerate the bonding process between you, your customers, your clients, associates, and especially those you are called to lead.

CHAPTER 6

COMEDY AND YOUR BRAND: HOW FAR IS TOO SOON?

I want to open this chapter by explaining its quirky, cryptic title, which I have crafted to show you why comedy is important in selling the truth (but must be used carefully). "Too soon!" is often what gets shouted out at comedy clubs when the comic jokes about something taboo, a recent tragedy, for example. There's a widely accepted formula contending that Comedy = Tragedy + Time. It accepts that part of comedy is the bad news, the uncomfortable truth, but that truth isn't funny unless it's presented the right way (and at the right time).

The fact is, truth tastes funny, reality is strange, and sometimes we have to laugh in the face of it in order to survive. So, this chapter endeavors to answer, "Why is comedy important in selling the truth?" and "How far can brands, businesses, teams, leaders, and organizations push comedy without offending or losing their audience?"

I'll set the stage for what we're going to talk about by sharing my own early experiences as a stand-up comedian and what I learned early on about using humor.

I first performed standup in 1991, a couple years out of college and while working for Carl Forsberg (see *Chapter 5*) repping commercial directors. My college buddy Steve Gold (of the Goldstar Talent Golds and now Sid Gold's Request Room in Chelsea, New York) knew the manager and got me a shot at the Comic Strip in New York City. This was to be a five-minute routine at around 1:30 a.m. (there were no open mics in those days). Even that late, the room was packed. I was about to go up when Eddie Murphy dropped in (he'd heard the room was hot). Eddie killed for 45 minutes, leaving behind a stunned crowd. So green was I that I didn't even watch Eddie's set—an utter failure on my part because it would have allowed me to play off the energy. The manager said, "Okay, kid, you're up." The late, legendary standup/actor Richard Lewis was standing in the archway as the manager said this, rubbing his forehead, massaging his trademark neuroses. He looked me in the eye. "I wouldn't do it," he said.

I did it.

I hadn't written any material at that point (something I'm glad I learned not to repeat in advance of the nazi bar show in the Valley; see *Chapter 3*). I had some voices and impressions in my quiver, but this was about getting up there. I'm so glad I got up there.

I bombed, to the best of my recollection. I did get a few laughs, but I was so green Kermit the Frog threatened to sue me for identity theft. I even did my version of standup improv, asking the audience for suggestions combining an impression and a situation. That led to me doing an impression of Mickey Rourke in an airplane bathroom. Yeah...

From that experience, I learned the cardinal rule of standup (and for everything else that I've done in business that's evolved around it): first, you gotta write. Doesn't matter whether it's the premise, or the words, whether you work it out on paper or onstage, *you must be prepared*. Don't wing it.

So, I started developing material, and the character of "Sonny Swing" emerged. He was the ultimate name-dropper and Bullshit artist, a cross between Jerry Lewis and Frank Sinatra. It clicked. I got on the radar of standup impresario Barry Katz and started playing the right rooms all over town. Only now does it occur to me that, just as I was inadvertently developing a career as a publicist, I was creating a stage persona who was a BS-er of epic proportions (i.e., "Oh, you like these socks? Thank Saddam Hussein." Or "You know you've made it when you're fighting over a hairbrush with Tony Bennett and Liza Minnelli.").

I certainly had great examples to follow. Comics emerging in the New York clubs about that time included Dave Attell, Dave Chappelle, Louis CK, Denis Leary, Jeff Ross, Colin Quinn, and Sarah Silverman. Everybody was trying to be as skilled as Seinfeld, as powerful as Kinison, as electric as Robin, as illuminated as Carlin, and as achingly real as Pryor. Today, we're just trying not to get slapped.

Years later, I have not become a standup insider. I'm an outsider with insider access and firsthand experience. I don't quite fit in anywhere. As a result, I've been all over the place, and at this point, rather than find my niche, I plan to roam until I've been everywhere.

This makes me a good observer, which is the second thing I learned from doing standup that is serving me well in my branding and business efforts: Good business is all about perspective—those of the brand, and its audience. Many comedians fail to put themselves in the shoes of the audience. They are in their own head, wrapped up in what they "have to say."

One of the ways I try to gain this perspective in my business and branding efforts is to gauge the sense of humor of a prospective client. What a person finds funny tells me a lot about their personality and offers a window into our prospective working relationship:

- How seriously do they take themselves?
- How open are they to constructive criticism?
- Are they prone to formality or informality?
- Are they comfortable in their own skin?
- Are they cautious, temperate, or bold?
- How attuned are they to subtlety and nuance?
- Do they stand in judgment of others?
- Do they hold prejudices?

And most importantly,

- How much fun are they to spend time with?

In going through this process, I'm not necessarily looking for clients who share my personal sense of humor. I'm just diagnosing their disposition so I can "size up the fit." Marc Maron is particularly skilled in this area, having cultivated his persona and audience via his seminal, long-running podcast, *WTF*. Knowing whether humor is going to come into play in your relationship, or not, can be important in your efforts to sell the truth in your branding and business activities. The practical determination you will make about humor is that a lack of it suggests a greater degree of fear, a more active ego, an unhealthy need for control, and a lack of receptiveness to input.

In business and in life, I think it is critical that you hone your receptors so that your humor is tuned to the funny bone of whatever customer, client, or audience you are trying to reach. Testing for humor can help you get the right perspective on anybody you want to win over. (So, now I may have answered the question you've had in your head since the beginning of this chapter: why on earth would I have included a chapter on using humor in a business book in the first place?)

The third truth stand-up comedy has taught me (and this is merely my unabashed, bold, and declarative personal opinion) is that you're never going to get where you wanna go unless you are *unapologetically audacious.* I will admit that I had to look up synonyms for "audacity" to discover that one of them is the Yiddish word, *chutzpah.* And in writing a chapter about comedy in business, humor is the nail, and chutzpah is the hammer—when to bring it down, and how hard, makes all the difference. Using humor the right way in business means never having to say you're sorry, never having to apologize for the truth when trying to sell it.

In standup, on the other hand, the point of comedy is to kill the audience, to hammer them to the point of the proverbial "mic drop." In the business world, when using humor, we still want to be audacious and bold, to "slay" our audience, so to speak, but not so brutal with the truth that it is off-putting. Simply put, in standup you can say anything you want as long as it's funny. In business, you have a different objective. You want to put the buyer at ease, make them comfortable with you and your point of view. The point of being bold in the way you use comedy in business is to win over your audience. Finding your voice and connecting with your audience isn't strictly about humor, of course, but laughter is visceral—it's as close to the truth as we can get without swallowing it whole. Comedy makes the truth more digestible.

KNOWING NO. 6: THE TRUTH SELLS BETTER WHEN IT TASTES BETTER, AND HUMOR IS A VERY EFFECTIVE WAY TO MAKE IT MORE PALATABLE

Where does humor play a role for you as an entrepreneur, as a leader? When it comes to personal branding, and brand voice across an organization, I encourage you to be as serious as possible at the outset. Comedy is a layer, and the firmer the foundation, the more useful that comedy will eventually be. So, foundationally, you build your brand on core values, unshakeable things. You set in stone what you stand for, and you make your promise earnestly. The stronger your spine, the more flexible your body. Only then can you start layering your messages with humor.

There's a reason they call it "making fun." We take something serious and impose a layer of irony over it, literally making it fun. It goes back to the axiom regarding experimentation in business: you must know the rules before you can break them. This is a good place to start when using humor in business, and it aligns with my belief that brands are built from the inside out. Once you are clear on who you are (see *Chapter 1*) and your values, you can shape your message, and you can use a variety of tools to do so—one of the most genius being humor—particularly when creating content for your ideal customer.

HOW COMEDY SHOULD BE USED TO SELL THE TRUTH

Those who are skilled in the sport can wield humor as a weapon, often fired in self-defense, able to pierce the heart of a target.

Depending on the circumstance, this can appear merciless, desperate, or hysterically funny.

To use humor correctly, there are a few things to keep in mind...

FIRST, DO NO HARM

Every brand (business, leader, idea) wants to stand out. But there are limits as to how far you can go to get that attention—remember, we don't want to push as far as a mic drop, only far enough that we know our intended audience is listening and can relate to the truth of our message.

Shock Jock radio from the 1990s comes to mind as an example of this. For years, I listened to Howard Stern during drivetime on Terrestrial Radio. I'm talking vintage Howard Stern, for whom no topic was off limits—the FCC-hounded, oft-fined Howard—not saintly, reflective, present-day Howard who weeps at the sight of Bruce Springsteen tickling the ivories live and in-person.

In 1997, how far you drove that humor nail in using the chutzpah hammer was pretty well-defined (and regulated). There were lines you didn't cross. Now, all lines have been crossed. Ironically, while common decency among elected officials is no longer maintained as a standard, entertainers must be careful not to offend, lest someone charge the stage and attack, or worse, cancel them. It's nuts.

At the same time, with hypocrisy on parade, business leaders, organizations, and brands have an opportunity to stand out by standing for something. But the way you stand up in defense of ideals is important. Do I stand up to poke fun at hypocrisy or criminality? Or do I limit my statements to positive affirmations about the principles in which I believe?

The most fundamental guideline I can provide for using humor to sell the truth is stolen from the ancient Greek physician, Hippocrates: *primum non nocere*, or "first, do no harm." Don't hurt nobody. Have fun. And not in a way that's really at anyone's expense. And, for G-d's sake, *learn to take a joke.*

I learned the importance of doing no harm when using comedy from my dad, who was a master at using humor to tell the truth about some rather serious things. I'm thinking of a particularly hilarious example of this when I was about 12. I'm sitting at the dinner table with my family (mom, dad, two older sisters). My oldest sister, Donna, is 17 at this point, and as she is the smartest of the three of us, her vocabulary has expanded considerably of late, most notably her use of the word, "shit." As in, "shithead," "full of shit," and "give a shit." The last one has endless variations, including, "Like I give a shit," "I could give a shit," and "Who gives a shit?" The bottom line: "I'm certainly not taking any shit from you."

So far, I've managed to control myself at the dinner table, remaining—as I remember it—the perfect boy. But on this night, some comment from someone elicits a "shit" from me. If I recalled exactly which variation was used, one would be left to wonder what significant memory was omitted to make room for that one. So, I don't know what I say exactly, but it's a "shitty" phrase.

My mom immediately expresses shock, with a multipurpose, "Hershel David!" She looks at my dad, who is expected to reprimand me and maintain the decorum and sanctity of our table. Our eyes meet. My dad knows the importance of decorum, he's a stickler for respect, even in jest, and yet, he also has impeccable comic timing. So, in this moment, he simply says, with an air of gentle admonition, "Come on, Heshy. That's no fuckin' way to talk."

This was a watershed moment. Not in terms of wanton profanity, but conversely, in terms of my standards for its use.

Not long after, my dad advised that profanity can be used to emphasize a point or break the tension, but should never be used in anger, or directed at an individual in any way that is derogatory or hurtful.

Remember, do no harm.

If you can dish it out as good as you get it, if you can spar with detractors in the light, without ever feeling compelled to deliver a fatal blow in self-defense, you win. This is where comedy in business and standup comedy part ways. A coup de gras—the mic drop—can indicate "killing" on stage, as I noted previously. A business doesn't set out to kill. A business seeks to win over its target audience, to build Know-Like-Trust (see *Chapter 5*) above all else, including laughs. Using humor to sell the truth in business is wonderful, so long as you do no harm.

Entertainment, engagement, and loyalty are the trifecta of brand strategy. We are not seeking to get laughs simply to get them, and any fun that we poke at our competitors should be good-natured. There's a warmth around comedy in business that highlights the advantages of our product or service without taking "cheap shots."

All of this is to say that for any pitfalls or risks associated with comedy, it is an indispensable tool, and the quickest way to establish an advantage over the competition.

To illustrate, let's examine one of the categories in which comedy dominates advertising: Insurance (think Progressive, Geico, Liberty Mutual, Farmers, Nationwide, Allstate). It all started with the Geico Gekko back in 1999 (created via The Martin Agency); it carried on through the Cavemen; Flo and the gang for Progressive (and the equally awesome and ongoing Dr. Rick campaign helping new homeowners keep from "turning into their parents"); Allstate's "Mayhem," the Allstate counter-weight of Dennis Haysbert; the wry J.K. Simmons for Farmers; and the list goes on and on and on.

What's being established in all these commercials? I mean, there are plenty of beer and alcohol ads that use humor, it's a common device. But insurance commercials are about trust—after all, you're trusting insurers with your home, your car, your *life*.

Here's my theory about why this seems to be the Golden Era of Insurance Comedy Advertising: in a post-truth world, sincerity is not enough. Sincerity demands that we accept something at face value. We no longer accept *anything* at face value—not even someone's face speaking directly to the camera, which could be a deep fake, for all we know. But comedy—*comedy* is the great equalizer. It doesn't beg for our belief. It's not proposing itself as a true statement of fact. It's a joke. It is up to *us* to see the truth in the statement. Comedy allows us to work some of it out for ourselves, and to make up our own minds, all while making the truth we hope to find in all of it more digestible. This demonstrates tremendous confidence in the product: we show that we take your concerns seriously enough, that we can laugh in the face of reality and back up our services in the process. Life may be ridiculous; our offer is not.

Which brings us to the lynchpin of comedy's effectiveness: intent.

INTENT

In part, intent is what makes a brand, business, or leader's attempt at humor worthy. Comedy comes down to a point of view. What is the tone and tenor of the joke? What is the intent? What is it releasing?

After all, comedy is about tension. It's a hold and release device. We pull back the bow as far as it will go, and if we release the punchline at the right moment, with proper aim, the arrow will hit its target.

Intent.

Let me illustrate what I mean by this with another story about Eddie Murphy. In his seminal 1987 concert film, *Raw*, he relates a story (in a flawless Cosby drawl) about the time Bill Cosby called to chastise him for using profanity in his shows. Offended, Murphy says he called the legendary Richard Pryor for his opinion. In his best Pryor voice, Murphy shares his mentor's reply: "Do people laugh when you say what you say?" Yes. "Do you get paid?" Yes. "Well, then, tell Bill to have a Coke and a smile and shut the fuck up!"

I am with Pryor on this. When it comes to comedy, the taste of the intended audience is what matters. You can't please everyone, nor should you try, and as long as you stay true to yourself, your brand, business, clients, and customers, those who love what you're selling will keep coming back.

Intent.

If your intent is clear, your audience will get the joke. Perfect example: one of the most beloved comedians in standup history, Don Rickles, aka "Mr. Warmth." His unparalleled ball-busting acumen belied an absolute sweetness that served to defang rather than bite.

My mom and grandmother once took a trip to Las Vegas and saw Rickles in concert. I remember my mother relating to us that there were a couple of Saudi gentlemen sitting in the front row, dressed in their traditional garb, including a thobe (robe) and shemagh (head covering). Rickles spotted them and called out, "Wow, look at the seats you got. No, that's great—come shoot a Jew-boy up close!" The room—Jews, Arabs, white, black, and all the rest—erupted in laughter. If there was any tension in the room before that joke, it was neutralized because the audience was equalized. Everyone knew that Rickles' intent was to put the entire audience at ease, including his Arab guests in the front row.

Sometimes, we use humor as a defense mechanism. We lash out. We fire back. It happens all day long amidst interpersonal conflicts. But it's not a preferred form of messaging. A little self-deprecation is better, and overall, the customer is the hero, not the product. The winning product serves the hero, it's an arrow in their quiver. So, whether we're releasing the tension as part of a literary thrill ride or pointing out the absurdity of prejudice to diffuse an awkward tension, there's the right time for humor. And as powerful a weapon as comedy is, it is surgical when we know how to use it.

By pulling back the curtain on comedy in this chapter, my hope is that you will be more apt to employ it, in business and life. For me, anyway, humor has been a saving grace, a survival mechanism, and my best friend. It's so close to our darkest realities because it must peer into the well of despair in order to lampoon it.

In writing about humor, I've hopefully softened the ground so we can talk about a touchier subject in the next chapter: money.

HOWARD RATNER
Uncut Gems

More than a dealer in gems, Howard Ratner is a remarkable odds-maker, known for his love of basketball. He is a member in good standing of The Diamond Dealers Club, the largest diamond trade organization in the world. His business affords him proximity to celebrities such as recording artist, The Weeknd, and he is so close to Kevin Garnett that the player once lent him his NBA Championship ring. A high point in his groundbreaking career is the extraction of a rare opal from an Ethiopian mine, where he employs miners who might otherwise struggle to make ends meet. The opal was estimated, at one point, to sell for up to one million dollars at auction.

Even amidst the usual chaos of separation, Ratner dotes on his children, compliments his wife, and makes time to attend family gatherings. His unbridled enthusiasm has on occasion resulted in a lost bet or two. At the same time, even his doubters must concede that his methods, while unusual, sometimes yield amazing results.

If Ratner is to be accused of trying to have it all, this is merely a testament to his passion, grit, and his firm belief that all things are possible.

⇜

The genius zone and the fun zone do not always align. That can make for some tricky decisions that can have a major impact on whether one stays in business or not. In the case of Howard Ratner, the antagonizing protagonist played by Adam Sandler in the 2019 American crime thriller, *Uncut Gems*, one could say that his genius zone collides with his fun zone, with mixed results. Howie makes one bad financial decision after another, complicated by the fact that, in many ways, he knows what he's doing. I often say that if people had encouraged me less, I would have given up show business. Less talent may have been a blessing. Howie is blessed with just enough smarts, drive, calculus, and audacity that he pushes that button when the smartest money is on holding back.

CHAPTER 7

HOW TO TURN DOWN
MONEY AND LIVE

L emme start off with a story about a disastrous moment in the
life of my company, affirming that it's possible to grow in the
wrong direction, and showing how growing in the wrong direction
may just be the right move.

The year was 2011, and after clawing my way back from a
recessionary slump, my niche PR firm was growing, with three
new partners from the worlds of finance, informatics, and web
development on board to help optimize the firm. The plan was to
grow even faster and to take the firm global with new offerings. Sure
enough, we landed a prospective client—an ad agency that would
represent about $150K per year in billings. The client was ours to
lose, and after our pitch meeting, the four of us headed back to the
office together. We rode in silence for a bit, checking our guts.

The upside: in terms of advertising industry PR (our niche), this was unquestionably a step forward, and we had the chops to serve the client in line with their expectations. The downside: our success relied on *their* creative, not ours, and we were not feeling the first campaign that was teed up for us to promote. This was their big break, in many ways, and securing favorable coverage in advertising trades would solidify our relationship with this agency over the coming year. To be clear, the campaign was for a humongous global brand, and it was certainly notable and worthy of consideration on that front alone. I'm pretty sure any other PR firm would have taken the gig and rolled the dice.

One of my partners broke the silence. "By a show of hands, who wants to take on this client?" Silence. And no hands. "Who wants to go to an open mic?" Four hands shot up without hesitation.

That was the moment we decided to turn down the money. Now, the big question was, would we still live? Well, let's not get ahead of the story too much just yet.

While I'd done standup at all the clubs in New York City in my 20s, my partners had never been on stage, other than to perhaps give a riotous toast at a wedding. So, the fact that they wanted to turn down the advertising dough in exchange for the dry mouth and stage fright of standup surprised me. It should not have. These three good men had gravitated to me not because of my facility with PR or brand strategy, but because of my creativity, and they wanted to experience it beyond the press releases and client meetings of agency work. They saw past the public relations niche to something I had been glimpsing only in the very furthest corners of my mind. Now, with their help, I was literally facing myself in the mirror, looking through my face into the inside lining against the back of my head and *seeing* it: the fact that performance is integral to my sense of usefulness.

For the next six months, we immersed ourselves in a new kind of PR—publicity for ourselves rather than big-name ad agencies. We put our performance and creativity skills out there in the rawest, most honest, and most vulnerable of ways: the standup comedy boot camp of open mics multiple times each week. We hustled ourselves all over LA, wherever we could find an open mic, getting three to five minutes of stage time apiece. We wrote and talked comedy in the office nonstop, breaking down the science of standup, scouring YouTube, and sharing clips of every notable comedian of the past 75 years. We became fixtures in the LA comedy scene, doing bringer shows at the Comedy Store, where we could watch the best comics in the world in any of three rooms on any given night.

Given my background, I thought I'd be the most advanced of the four of us. I wasn't. My partner, Ernie Noh, was a natural. He kind of exploded onstage, having waited so long to get up there. He hated writing so we provided support, but his presence was undeniable.

While we were still servicing our clients, we were also obsessed with standup. There was a method to this madness: we reasoned that we could add branded comedy to our repertoire, transitioning into more of a creative agency than merely a PR firm. This evolution had begun a few years earlier before we officially partnered, two of us acting as freelance creative directors in the athletic sneaker industry and having some success with viral videos (which employed well-targeted humor) for brands like Reebok and PF Flyers.

Trouble was, we bought into the idea that to become experts at standup comedy, we needed to streamline our client roster and invest in comedy development, production, and performance. I'd always hedged my bets, and it could be argued (and was at the time) that my failure to launch as a standup and mainstream screenwriter was due to my lack of total commitment and aversion to risk. So, this time I went "all-in," which resulted in wins, for sure: we became good standups, good enough to work. We built strong relationships with clubs and up-and-coming comics. And we produced a Honda spec spot (a speculative commercial created independently of the featured brand, meaning with our own money) that garnered twice the views the brand's official "viral" video had generated.

But we were a bit out of control, to say the least. We needed a roadmap for our reinvention, and we needed a dispassionate bean counter to keep us in line. Instead, we were four all-ins, with no "hold-on" voices in the mix. Ernie was the designated CFO, and here's a big lesson: he wasn't a numbers guy. He'd said to me, "I sell investment portfolios; I'm not a CFO. I'm a risk-taker, so I can promise you I'll be bold." I only heard "risk-taker" and "I'll be bold." The bit about not being a CFO went right past me. I loved Ernie (and still do). When he dressed like a CFO, man, did he look and act the part. But he wasn't a bean counter. Three of us had wives and at least two children (four, in my case). Our wives were voices of reason and support, and we guzzled the support while ignoring the reason.

We also guzzled a lot of booze. I'd worked on Madison Avenue in the early 90s, hearing stories about the previous decades' debauchery, but that was winding down by the time I got there. Now, in a "Mad Men" frenzy, we were living out the three-martini-lunch fantasy by day and the smoky whiskey-and-coke vibe of the comedy scene by night. Uber made a killing on us.

But when we pried our eyes open, we were broke. And by choice(!). We'd invested in everything from production to technology (including viable software projects inside and outside the comedy realm). The problem wasn't the ideas, it was that we were trimming our roster of good paying clients in order to focus on the future of where we hoped to take our PR firm.

We were, in many ways, victims of our own aptitude. People gave us more chances than we deserved, based on our track records of dependability, diligence, smarts, and creativity. We'd never gone off any deep end before. And we were good. Our shows were good. Our new comedy relationships were golden and remain so to this day. But the *balance* was off.

So, when I say you can turn down money and live—to regret it—the paradox is apt. Should we have taken on that big agency client? Probably not. Should we have gone "all-in" on standup? Well, in terms of commitment, I would not take back one open mic, bar show, or lineup I was in. But I could have done those things while maintaining my existing roster of business, if I'd understood the benefits of balance and the pitfalls of absolutes.

Because of our absolutist all-in approach, we gambled and lost. The revenue we'd sacrificed was not replaced by profits from our comedy and tech endeavors (nor was it reasonable to think we would see a return so quickly), and it all kind of fell apart. We folded our company, losing a handful of truly talented young professionals whom we had been mentoring and nurturing. While it's awesome to see how far they've come since, we missed out on the chance to do some great work with the next generation of marketing talent.

As we wrapped up our "All-in Brotherhood of the Wandering Comics," I took a hiatus from drinking. I dropped 15 pounds, and the comparisons shifted from Nathan Lane (who I love) to Robert Downey, Jr. (who I also love, though he's an ectomorph, so if I get to choose a comparison...). I continued to do standup shows, and not surprisingly, they were much better. I performed in a benefit show featuring songs from Disney movies performed exclusively by Broadway artists. I was the only non-Broadway artist there and was glad to feel that I held my own.

I returned to my niche of client-driven PR and freelance copywriting as an independent contractor, but I was still seeking ways to monetize my performance chops. Standup was not the answer. I had my chance to go on the road when I was 23. Doing so in my late 40s was not the play.

Creatively, I was energized. In 2016, I partnered with good friend and repeat client Stu Wilson to create content and a pilot for *The Tiny Sirko Show*, in which I starred as a bad boy exec who reinvents himself as a Ukrainian little person "fleeing the dogs of Vladmir Putin." I wrote the pilot script for a comedy-drama streaming series called *Smithereens*, about an alcoholic amnesiac who may be a hit man or a standup comedian, depending on how you interpret the flashbacks. It was a finalist in both the LA Comedy Fest and Beverly Hills Film Festival.

Meanwhile, I resumed creative marketing for the footwear industry, which reunited me with good friends (one of whom was a partner in the All-In Brotherhood of the Wandering Comics fiasco). With our client in Asia (which I had never visited previously), I was able to travel to Thailand, Japan, China, and Taiwan. This work helped ease financial pressures, and from there, a new boutique agency—Propeller 5—was born, with me as CCO (chief creative officer) and my frequent partner, iconic indie retailer Isack Fadlon, as CEO.

Despite the 2020 pandemic, in 2021 we managed to develop The KOSHER Brand, a streetwear apparel brand rooted in kindness, equity, and inclusivity. I threw myself into the endeavor with everything I had. The experience put me in touch with my purpose. While it is a for-profit company, I led the charge in establishing The Keep It Kosher Project, supporting street artists working to share positive messages throughout their communities. We officially launched in 2022, and time will tell where the KOSHER journey takes us. At this writing, we are seeking the right person to shepherd the brand into profitability. We have put all the pieces together and injected the brand with honesty, integrity, and heart so that it radiates the positronics of its DNA—and I have no doubt that there are great things to come.

The professional takeaway I gleaned from all of this? "Keep it simple, stupid," which brings us to Knowing No. 7:

KNOWING NO. 7: BALANCE IS WHAT KEEPS THE PIECES ON THE BOARD

This means that whatever you do, workwise and personally, and whatever risks you take in work and in your important relationships, remember to control the board, keep things in balance.

One of the ways I have learned to maintain that balance is to stop labeling myself and others. I used to think each person was a certain thing or type. "She's practical," or "They're adventurous," or "He's a comedian."

But that simplistic labeling is a copout. It's too easy. As an artist, I certainly tried my hand at it with plenty of "I can't" and "I'm not good at that," or "That's not my thing." Sure, there are roles we do not wish to play, and we should seek out those things that make us happy. But the deepest joy comes from *seeking to be a whole person,* and that may very well require expanding our view of just what we are capable of and what others can bring to the table.

My TV pilot script, *Smithereens*, reflected my feelings of hyper-segmentation, the different roles I was playing in my life, some of them conflicting, others confusing, some synergistic, some completely at odds:

Comedian

Father

Husband

Publicist

Partner

Copywriter

Brother

Worshipper

Leader

Follower

Confidant

Son

Prince

Creative Director

Victim

Pauper

Powerhouse

Cynic

Believer

But the main role I played was:

Worrier.

In all that disjointed displacement, I'd grown comfortable wondering and worrying about my "role" in life, about who I really was trying to be. I was a walking contradiction, awaiting resolution. I thought I had to make a *choice* somehow, that it had to be one or the other: Doctor or lawyer? MD or JD? Artist or professional? MFA or MBA? I didn't see that my superpowers (each of us has at least one, probably more) didn't have to be restricted to what that power entails. Our superpower isn't just the thing we're really good at—it's the thing *behind* the thing we're really good at; it's the *purpose* of the thing. Thus, that superpower can translate very nicely across a variety of roles in our lives, since we are the sum-total of our conflicting parts. Additionally, we must learn how best to lead, associate, stand, and deliver. Let's examine the following formula: Lead + associate + stand + deliver = balance, and how it serves us in a post-truth world.

LEAD

I've spent a good deal of time up to this point talking about the best ways to lead in business, branding, and building company culture. It involves knowing that there is a discoverable truth that we can all rely on as an ally in an age of relativity and confusion. It also requires that we get real with ourselves, know who we are and what our own personal brand stands for. It means not tolerating any sort of lying from ourselves or others. All of this results in better leadership and makes the business risks we face much less deadly.

ASSOCIATE

When you get into your 50s, it's easy to say to yourself, "I don't need any new associates." I've said it many times in the past. I already have a group of close friends and colleagues who are loving, loyal, supportive, inspiring, and fun. Nothing can top 20 years or more of close camaraderie. But timing is its own animal. And nothing can top being open to new associations, where colleagues with similar values and goals are appreciated and we can join forces to raise all ships. However, I did recognize that, at times, professionally speaking, my world was too small, too niche, and to best associate with likeminded business leaders, I would need to do some work on my mindset (see *Chapter 8)*. I had to replace doubt with *listening*...listening to myself, to the universe. Doing so has created better balance in my life and made taking the risks of life much easier.

STAND

Another thing I had to do to create better balance was stand on my own. In the past, I had partnered or invited partners into every endeavor I'd undertaken. It always worked out to some extent, then stalled, failed, or malfunctioned. I wrongly assumed that I was an incomplete businessperson. I didn't like numbers or operations, and that's fair enough. But in shying away from certain tasks, I put the onus of success on other people, which was unfair and ill-advised. I'm a born collaborator, a team player, and a very good leader, but I don't need partners. I need a team. I need to surround myself with amazing humans who understand their own superpowers, their own purpose and are superstars in their own right. I need accountability partners to keep me honest. But the buck has to stop with me.

DELIVER

I learned that it is up to me to deliver the goods. That was after I took an in-depth Peak Performance course (more on this in the next chapter), where I learned that I need to take my fate into my own hands. I don't know what I intended to get out of the course when I enrolled, but I knew I had to progress personally and professionally, so I decided to start with this training.

The course allowed me to consider what I wanted to deliver to my family, friends, associates, team members, and audience. It also gave me my first taste of "community" in the virtual sense. At the time, I took the course in 2021, things were finally opening up travel-wise, but I knew I did not want to resume the same niche marketing schedule of events I had participated in pre-pandemic. If I did, I really could not control the flow of business. It would be a hit and miss pursuit, reliant on a single community and the deliverables of my agency.

Things were good businesswise in 2021, but financially, 2022 was shaping up to be my worst year ever. To distract myself, I followed the same pattern I always had, and began developing a creative property, a musical-comedy cabaret. Sounds like a real moneymaker, doesn't it? This was no way to deliver, but I hadn't come to terms with that about myself just yet. The show was called *Truth Tastes Funny*, and one of my closest and most talented friends, the brilliant music producer Steven M. Gold, loved the idea and was advising me on the show's development. I'd thought through the "long game," which involved a New York run, a tour, a book, and more. But in truth, I was taking the path of least resistance. I knew it would be a great show, with a great message, but could I project the revenue it would generate? Of course not. I was hiding again, avoiding long-term reality, lying to myself just a bit. On some level, I knew it. This was no way to sell the truth, no way to deliver on the expectations I had of myself.

Eventually, I switched gears and was able to deliver with my *Truth Tastes Funny* podcast, which is now in its fifth season. It's pretty much in line with this chapter since it's all about choices, turning down money, misappropriating resources, committing, over-committing, indulgence, balance, failing, giving credence to knowing, growing in the wrong direction, and moving in the right direction. It's also about the uselessness of regret. Howard Ratner's Legit Bio, with which I began this chapter, showcases the fact that Ratner doesn't wallow in regret—I'm not even sure he can relate to it. Ratner instinctively knows that regret doesn't tell you what you need at this moment. It doesn't even keep you from making the same mistakes. **Spoiler Alert:** "Uncut Gems" came out five years ago, but just in case you haven't seen it, skip over the following paragraph and see the film as soon as you can:

My point is, Howard dies in the end. And his demise has nothing at all to do with luck or the all-or-nothing bet he placed. In fact, he won the bet. But his manner, his personality, his refusal to give an inch in human interaction, his compulsion to push blindly—to *push* his luck—leads one of the ruthless crooks with whom he's gotten mixed up to shoot him in the head. Balance—equilibrium—would have led to a happier ending.

Okay, keep reading...

What outcome do you want? Whatever outcome you're after, I advocate for a balanced strategy. Equal parts leadership, association, independence, and performance. Extreme commitment is not a strategy. I've invested more money in this phase of my career than I have invested cumulatively up to this point. I am undoubtedly, unabashedly, audaciously, all-in on my game plan for the next five to ten years. My tactics may shift, my schedule is certainly fluid. I will likely add or remove elements as I go (ABT – Always Be Testing!). But I have been brave enough to look at the board from many perspectives. I've sought counsel where I might otherwise have "trusted my gut" and commitment alone.

The courage to see the world as it is a core tenet of selling the truth. Proper perspective—aka balance—paves the way for successful experiments. And as we'll discuss in the next chapter, it helps us accept that the breakthrough is in our head, not the wall we're banging it against.

ADELAIDE WILSON & RED
Us

Parenthood is not easy under the best of circumstances. Leading the way for the next generation of moms are two ferociously determined women: Adelaide Wilson and Red. The sunny town of Santa Cruz, California, is home to just over 60,000 people, but many, many more spend their summers on the boardwalk, the beach, or out on the water. As children, Adelaide and Red shared a "moment" under that very boardwalk, in a funhouse (depending on your idea of fun), that changed both of their lives.

When Adelaide and Red are reunited—each of them now married, with a son and daughter—it becomes clear they have more in common than sets them apart. For every problem, there is a solution. For every conflict, a resolution. And while their struggle shines a light on larger social issues, in the big picture, the story of Adelaide and Red is about patience, planning, and living your best life.

❧

Jordan Peele's 2019 thriller, *Us*, is a tale of trauma, doppelgangers, power dynamics, societal bloodletting, privilege, interpersonal relationships, and more. With its twist ending (if you haven't watched the film…*watch the film!*), it's also a lesson in perspective.

Depending on your perspective, neither Adelaide nor Red are villains and both may be heroes. Yet each must kill to survive. And while each demonstrates the ability to show grace, only one has the innate ferocity to save her family and claim victory. Takeaway? There's a time to be nice, and a time to gut the opposition with a pair of golden shears.

CHAPTER 8

THE BREAKTHROUGH IS IN YOUR HEAD (NOT THE WALL)

The word "mindset" is something I often equate with bullshit, lumping it in with all the other phony baloney semantics of business-speak that popped up in the 90s and have hung on in everyone's speech for how long now? Likely you have used the word, along with others such as "woowoo" and "new-agey," throwing them out as slurs against false prophets, mediums, spiritual healers, 3-card monte hustlers, snake oil salesmen, and anyone who tries to "sell me what I already know." Like me, you've probably deposited such people in the same basket, which you have labeled, "People trying to screw me out of something" (see *Chapter 4)*. Prior to the Summer of 2021, I would have done the same. But, beginning that July, I really did change my "mindset," and this chapter chronicles that journey in hopes of helping you perhaps make your own perspective shifts in your efforts to optimize your own success.

Even now, I am not trying to sell you on anything other than the truth, which is that if you are willing to let go of some things you don't need, you leave your mind free to take in some things that have eluded you thus far. And in a book titled *Selling the Truth*, there's nothing wrong with adding a little more on that topic wherever seems appropriate, so here I go.

Sometimes, ignoring the truth becomes a habit. We're frightened of changes that might come from facing reality, so we go down the same road again and again, not getting the results we're after. We would do better to examine why we think we want what we think we want and what we might really want. It's possible we actually *do* want what we think we want, but the important point I want to make here is that the *examination just may lead to a new approach*. And we ultimately have to *sell* others on our mission in order to accomplish it. So, let's make darned sure that our mission is crystal clear to us. Confidence sells. Uncertainty…well, I'm not sure if uncertainty does *anything*.

Sometimes, uncertainty is manifested in our obstinance, or in other words, our close ties to the wrong outcome. We secretly know that this thing we want isn't the thing we should be after (but don't know why), and thus we fear illumination. After all, illumination can bring about a lot of hard work.

Imagine, for instance, that you are in a dark room. You have little space in which to move about. Only a sliver of light shines on the corner of a stone object. You try to get your hands around the object but can't quite get a grip on it. Certainly, you cannot move the object. Not much to do there in that dark room.

Now, picture the same room bathed in light, emanating from a high-placed window. The floor is littered with boxes. They're packed pretty tightly together, which is why you felt cramped. With some effort, you can lift one of the boxes and make more room for yourself to operate. You also see that the stone object is a small step, and reason that if you stack the boxes properly, you can build a stairway to the window. And from there, you can perhaps examine what lies beyond.

The difference between the dark room and the room that is illuminated isn't really the light. It's that once you can see, you must make a choice regarding how you will act from there. You could stay confined, continually bumping up against the boxes, yet somewhat comfortable in your known frustration (you can't be blamed for not knowing what you're really dealing with in the dark room). Or you can use the boxes to make stairs and climb to the window, where you can finally see other options, free to imagine new possibilities. If you are having a hard time getting anywhere in your cramped, dimly lit room, perhaps it's time to embrace the light.

KNOWING NO. 8: IF GETTING THERE IS SO HARD, ASK YOURSELF IF YOU NEED A SHIFT IN PERSPECTIVE SO YOU CAN SEE WHERE YOU REALLY WANNA GO

This Knowing is about flexibility. You can stop worrying that you're "settling" for less if you finally have the courage to examine whether the processes you have been following are really serving you. What if these so called "tried-and-true" processes are nothing more than head-banging, inflexible, unproductive methods that need some serious re-examining? This opens you up to some wonderful breakthroughs. It helps you see that perhaps your current strategies are flawed, and that your desired outcomes (which could even be something wonderfully important and meaningful) are fundamentally wrong for you. Ultimately, they are not even really *you*.

When you are willing to take on a new mindset, you begin to realize that you no longer need to glom onto a handful of very finite outcomes, and instead visualize several different possibilities for reaching your potential. In fact, while "meeting your potential" has a nice ring to it, "Testing the boundaries of your potential" is even better. And "Testing the boundaries of your potential to positively affect the world you share with others" is really nice. However you want to term it, you will begin to see that you may have been making things much harder than they need to be (in all your efforts to reach some grandiose purpose you thought you should be pursuing) and see the repeated futility of that unnecessarily difficult path. These repeated outcomes of failure and head-banging are an indication that you are, indeed, not headed in the right direction. Isn't this the quintessential definition of insanity? Are there pathways you could be exploring instead and are not because you are so tied to certain outcomes? Consider that today there are options and ways of doing things that perhaps never occurred to you 10 years ago, 10 months ago, or even 10 days ago when you got it settled in your head that you needed to achieve something by going down only one very specific pathway.

This chapter is about being willing to let go of those mindsets— things you don't need any longer—and instead imagine places in your head you have never allowed yourself to go before. It's about proving to yourself that you can break down the walls that have prevented you from seeing new possibilities. The breakthrough should be in your mind, not the wall you have been banging your head against for so long.

Throughout the rest of this chapter, I want to discuss some of the walls on which I have left a heavy imprint and show you how I broke the habit. Perhaps you can relate to some of these walls as well (and be thinking about the other walls not mentioned here that you have often come up against).

WALL OF G-D

I have been a dreamer and a fantasist since I was a kid. I loved movies, theater, music, storytelling, comedy, and art—any medium in which I could fabricate, anything I could draw outside the lines. But in life, I was sheltered and cautious, as though the "stage" was where liberation and joy were found. That fantastical world was safe because it *wasn't* real, but it also felt pretty close sometimes.

As wild as my imagination was, my actual life was neatly constrained within the strictures of Orthodox Judaism. One could substitute almost any religion, but the common denominator that often leads us to bang our head against the Wall of G-d is the prohibitive upbringing that trains us to fear the unknown and accept the answer, "Because this is how we do it."

I had faith in the form of organized religion—it was something you put in G-d, not man, and the boundaries were clearly defined. I love Judaism and am so happy and proud to have been born into a belief system that is at once logical and requiring interpretation, with an emphasis on "Tikun Olam"—repairing the world—and loving humankind. While I have struggled with religious constructs and tend to reject extreme or absolute notions, I treasure the depth of wisdom and goodness inherent in Judaism. I also gleaned my "Truth Tastes Funny" perspective from being Jewish. As Lawrence J. Epstein notes of Jewish comedians in America in his phenomenal book, *The Haunted Smile*, "The comedians offered audiences consolation through laughter in times of distress…They bound diverse members of the American community to one another; Americans who could laugh together didn't fight. Finally, the comedians gave their audiences a weapon, characteristically satire, to confront life's unfairness."

I ultimately found my spiritual self in the unlikeliest of spots: Iowa City. Removed from judgment, and in a small, tight-knit community representing every conceivable level of Jewish practice, I was at once comfortable and out of water. I discovered that when all the fish are out of water, we are more positively disposed to finding the river together.

WALL OF MONEY

If you haven't guessed by now, making money is not my superpower. And I'm not sure what role money plays in your goal stack, either. I do know that I respect it much more than I used to.

In any event, another wall that I continually banged my head against was money—not how to get it, but how to welcome it into my life and make it work for me. A major step towards knocking this wall down was joining the Peak Performance community, Zero2Dangerous (Z2D). I say "community" instead of "course," because while it is a course—an intensive one—the people who had taken the course previously, and who were still around in the community, taking it again, sharing insights, continuing to grow, were the most important take-away for me. Yes, I needed to change my work habits. But I also needed to meet new people (see the Associate subsection at the end of *Chapter 7* for more on this) and compare notes on the journey of life. Most importantly, I needed to *invest money in my own success*. Because much of my business has come from people hiring me to write and advise, I've been able to keep my overhead low. But you get out what you put in, and if I wanted to realize my earning potential, I would have to level up.

At the point I enrolled in Z2D, investing $4,000 was a big deal, but something inside me recognized that the transformation I had in mind could not be accomplished alone. I needed outside perspectives, new ideas, and some tough love. I was right. I would roll the dice again in 2022, my worst year ever in terms of revenue (for real, I don't think I'd made that little money since the recession in 2009 or when I was working at a computer store in 1993), investing in podcasting and dropping (borrowing) $10K for a mastermind class that was at its core one big step-up sales pitch. Yet the connections I made there transformed my game. It was not what it purported itself to be, but it was the right move. It propelled me to the next step.

WALL OF THE MIND

In the Peak Performance community, I was privileged to meet a person who was likewise searching for a "better way" to achieve satisfaction in business; she introduced me to the notion of Human Design. She shared charts and numbers, stuff I could hardly follow, but the point is, I was *open* to the *idea* that I may have been—as I alluded to in the previous chapter—growing in the wrong direction, going against the grain of my true self, to my financial detriment. That got me thinking about an easier way out of the head-banging...

...I could see myself making a short film called "The Diagnosis," in which a young man or woman sits in a doctor's office adorned with degrees in neuroscience from Pretentious University, a citation from the Board of SuchandSuch, and honored as a Fellow in Thisandthat. All the right credentials. The doctor enters, white coat and the whole schmear, and proceeds to educate the patient on human design, quantum consciousness, and maybe scalar light healing, ultimately writing a prescription for total fulfillment in the form of Abundisone (20 mg) and Prosperizam (10 mg) twice daily for the first two weeks, upped to 40 mg and 20 mg, respectively, thereafter. Would you take the meds, assuming the side effects were minimal, and did not include incontinence, drunk driving, or suicidal ideation? I would. I couldn't help but go there in my mind.

But back to the real story and the real work...

In addition to the Human Design concept, I also heard a lot about using meditation while in Peak Performance, something I had never done prior. One of my dear friends and mentors, the CEO of a world-renowned heritage footwear brand, had begun meditating for three minutes each day and found it transformative. But yoga, meditation, these things seemed foofy to me. Who has time to sit quietly for three minutes? Well, if you've spent 90 minutes watching an action movie pairing Mark Wahlberg with a comedian, that's 30 meditation sessions right there. Which one will make you more money? Even if you're in the film business, there's no wrong answer. But think about it.

So, I gave meditation a whirl, got the Headspace app, and over the next several months, it calmed me down, eased my anxiety in stressful moments, and allowed me to progress as a professional (and creative) creature. Sometimes, I felt guilty jumping up to write down business ideas or notes mid-meditation, but meditation strongly advises against guilt over poor meditation practices. I suspect I'm not alone in breaking the zen moment to reflect on or write down thoughts that come from being in a totally illuminating headspace.

Also, my Peak Performance routine called for me to rise at 5 a.m. daily. This was fine with me since I'm an early bird, not a night owl, but I got up so early that meditating at night often ended up putting me to sleep, leading to a little more guilt. But I've outgrown the guilt. I now use meditation to lull me to sleep at night, or back to sleep when necessary, and it takes less than five minutes.

The point is, using meditation, I have broken down many of the walls I had put up in my head, and now see things differently in my mind than I ever have before. I have grown (and slimmed down a little, but that's another story). This is the irrefutable truth, and herein is the groundwork I laid for my material success. Not in the form of a pill (as I had fantasized in my short film), but in the form of positive thinking and courage, backed up by some hard f-ing work.

So, positive thinking. Regardless of my human design (I believe I'm a "reactor," and knowing this has changed my entire approach to business, because I now realize "creating" for me does not exist without "reacting") and my improved work ethic, I still felt there was a barrier between me and the money I wanted to earn. For some reason, I was pushing money away, or at least facing the wrong direction as it was flying toward me.

But then came my *Truth Tastes Funny* podcast. And it was through TTF that I found Janet Elaine Schmidt.

I could have called this chapter "Quantum Consciousness Accelerators I Have Known"—and maybe I'll use that as a subhead— but the thing to take away is that until I met Janet, "quantum consciousness" and "goal balances" and "epigenetic imprinting" were not words I would ever have put together. However, by the time I welcomed Janet to *Truth Tastes Funny*, I had immersed myself in a monthslong Peak Performance course, explored human design, meditated regularly for a year, interviewed a dozen diverse humans with dozens more potential solutions to life's crazy challenges, and—perhaps this is the lynchpin—grown tired of *wanting* but never really *welcoming* success.

It was time to change my mindset, from one of wanting and waiting, to welcoming and winning.

My interview with Janet on *Truth Tastes Funny* offers insight into her skills, qualifications, narrative, and process. It also allows you to hear/watch me become aware of this field in real time. What really matters is that her appearance on my show was followed by two sessions with Janet, in which we replaced unproductive beliefs with beliefs far more conducive to success and happiness. There was a time, not so long ago, when I'd prefer turn-by-turn instructions to a road map, i.e., "Just tell me what to do to get there." Well, that's changed, and it is my hope that this book reflects that change: it is all about opening minds and hearts to affect change in our lives and the world at large.

What I have achieved in this recent leg of my journey is a healthy balance between reality and possibility, with the decks cleared of self-pity and undue self-deprecation. Any progress is not attributable to any one step. Yet, I did begin it all with the Peak Performance course with its emphasis on crafting a "Massive Transformative Purpose (MTP)." Big words—and yes, it's meant to be a big statement. My MTP has evolved over time, but basically as long as I'm willing to break down walls and take a look at things from angles that might have been hidden from me in the past. All the cups seem to fall into place to create a taller and taller goal stack, possibilities I may or may not pursue, but which I can now imagine as options I would never have considered before. This has become my truth, one which has integrity behind it to the point I can sell it not only to others, but most importantly, to myself.

FAUXTHENTICITY, DON'T FAIL ME NOW!

Just as it sounds, "fauxthenticity" refers to false authenticity. Meaning, fake. Why don't I just say "fake"? Because it's more than that, it's a commentary on the overuse of the word "authenticity" in today's marketing vernacular. We hear how "Gen Z craves authenticity," as I mentioned in Chapter 1, which we all know has a kernel of truth but is laughable in the sense that it implies the rest of us crave bullshit.

But forget for a moment what we crave. It may not be about what we crave, but rather what we aspire to. Do we aspire to reckon with reality, or would we prefer to live out our days being full of shit and continue banging our head against the wall as well? (I will discuss with my editor whether to substitute symbols for the offending "i"s above, but I do not feel they are gratuitous in the slightest.) Circling back to the benefits of the many avenues I explored over the past several years, the fruit of those labors is the knowledge that it's possible to evolve our mindset, and that saying something is authentic doesn't make it so. We must do the work. And herein lies the lynchpin of this chapter: Doing the work is hard, but it leads somewhere. So, if I bang my head against the wall and never break through, I'm making life harder than it needs to be. While if I take the time and effort to change the way I think about things, to question my purpose and destiny, it will be costly, rife with trial and error, but I will progress. And it will be worth it, no matter the outcome in the short term.

Changing your mindset is a four-step process:

1. Recognize that perhaps you are stuck in a cramped, dark room.
2. Realize you will need to find a reliable light source to help illuminate the room.

3. Prepare yourself emotionally for a shift in perspective once you see what's actually in the room.
4. Shift your perspective by being unafraid of imagining more than what you thought was there before things became clearer.

Keep in mind that when that perspective shift takes place your relationship with the truth will evolve—usually, for the better. If you can figure out what compels you to act like a pirate, for instance, you can figure out if that, indeed, is your brand and what you really want to sell to others. Of course, it isn't enough to act like yourself. You need to be yourself to really sell the package.

Believe it or not, we have covered eight of the nine Knowings of selling the truth! What we haven't asked yet is what's the point of all this self-examination, personal development, toil, and success? What do we do with our well-gotten gain?

I believe it is to leave a legacy.

But what do I mean by "legacy?" I used to worry what my legacy would be like, what I would leave behind for my children. But I've discovered that's all a moot point. A legacy isn't just an inheritance we leave to our children. It's what we are, and it will be left regardless of our consideration on the matter. Our legacy is the sum-total of our actions over the course of our lives. What kind of a legacy will it be?

That's a question for the concluding chapter, where we will explore what this truth telling and selling is all for.

SPOILER ALERT: YOU ARE A LEGACY BRAND

Opinions vary regarding the appropriate length for a serious nonfiction business book. Some say it should be 40,000 words. Others suggest 50,000 to 60,000 words. I did an internet search on the "appropriate length for a funny nonfiction semoir about business," and got basically the same numbers, with the addition of: "Does not include: funny or semoir." Maybe the best guide for a book's length ought to come from the notion that the longer the book, the less your reader learns. So, I'm thinking now is a good time to wrap this up—I want you still wishing I would keep going with the jokes as I take my bow, rather than nervously fiddling with your car keys, hoping I'll walk off stage already.

Regardless of the book's length, you have come a long way with me, so I hope it's not too much to ask that you come just a little further and read this concluding chapter in the context of your whole self. We're in pretty deep by now, so hopefully the value that you find in my stories and observations applies across the board for you, regardless of whether you are at a pivotal moment in your professional journey, doing some serious self-reflection, or having a complete existential crisis (some may call it an opportunity).

So, here's the crux of this concluding chapter and the ninth Knowing, which just happens to be the most important of them all:

KNOWING NO. 9: YOU ARE A LEGACY BRAND

What do I mean by this?

The impact we have on the world becomes our brand. How we are perceived both now and after we're gone… this is the legacy we leave to others. This legacy brand is something we will have cultivated—knowingly or unknowingly—over the course of our mortal lives. Here's hoping like hell it's a good one, right? Whatever brand you leave to others as your legacy depends largely on how much you have valued the truth, and whether you were able to sell that truth with a pure heart, both professionally and personally.

MY DAD AND THE MEANING OF "LEGACY"

I was 29 years old when my father passed away, and only now am I truly processing the loss. At the shiva we held for him, I asked my late uncle, the revered Rabbi Sholom Rephun, what becomes of us when we die. After all, if the brain dies, so do our memories and our knowledge of life on earth. My uncle shared that while Judaism does not embrace the notion of "Heaven" or "Hell," we do believe strongly in the viability of the soul, the "Neshama," which does carry on. The Neshama has been impacted by all its experiences in the living world. In fact, we "sit shiva" in the home of the deceased because in the aftermath of death their soul is in turmoil, being pulled away from their physical existence. The presence of loved ones and the familiar environment eases the soul's path forward, and wherever it goes next, this soul will retain an imprint from this world. Thus, the ultimate connections we make are beyond words, beyond the material, and are the essence of our time here.

Although I had begun the discussion with my uncle asking questions about the "afterlife," what we were really talking about was my father's legacy. Every interaction my dad had with me had imprinted his Neshama with part of my soul, and reciprocally, these interactions had left their imprint on my soul. For those of us still here in the physical world, this represents an opportunity to carry forward all the good things that have been impressed upon us—and to create deep connections that will have an impact not only now, but also in the future.

So now, I need to ask something of you in terms of these connections you are making and the impact that they will have on you and those you care deeply for, which is, at this very moment, creating your legacy brand. The problem is, I'm not good at asking for things. It's uncomfortable. It's awkward. It feels one-sided and thus unfair. I'm getting antsy just thinking about it. However, I'm fairly certain I can do it, since in this case I'm not asking you to do something for me. I'm asking you to do this for you, for your brand, and for your legacy.

Here's my ask. It's just three simple words: *Change your life*.

Yes, change your life using the Nine Knowings of selling the truth that we have explored throughout this book:

Shift.

Dig.

Upheave.

Change your business model.

Maybe change industries.

Move. To another city, or another country maybe.

Make new friends.

If you have it, spend it. Spread it around.

Disentangle yourself.

Become entangled.

Disengage with what doesn't make you happy.

Set your clock to fulfillment.

Drop out of society!

Don't take yourself too seriously.

And last but certainly not least... invite more humor.

Hold on. I should have said this before I hurled all that at you, but please do all of this *in your mind* first. Try it out as an exercise, then decide where you really need to make a change. Because after reading this book, you should be at your optimum connecting point to what's true for you. This is the moment where your personal life and your professional brand are the most in sync. After doing this exercise, I hope you will emerge with a real desire for change and a hunger for freedom (which is just another word for truth, in my opinion). So, maybe we should include something here about freedom of choice in terms of creating a legacy brand we can be proud of.

FREE WILL

There are many ways in which we may be constrained. Whether we're coloring inside the lines (something I could never be found guilty of... "Oh geez, Hersh, there you go again, outside the lines!"), filling out forms, consenting to the appropriation of our data, determining the number of words our book should have, applying for a job, or even meditating, it's possible to relinquish our free will. The "religiously organized" among us often struggle to reconcile G-d's omniscience with our own free will. In other words, if G-d decides our fate (a reason to pray *for* something), how does our own will factor into it?

Okay, I'm not touching that one with a ten-foot staff.

But I will say that even with all the angst about where our freedom to choose ends and where the will of the Universe takes over, we still need to remember that we are not cogs in a machine to be acted upon. We are here to get into it deeply, using our own abilities to think and reason. Let the Divine Rabbit (however we refer to a power beyond our control) worry about what all that free-thinking is doing to us! We must be more like Billy Hayes, from Alan Parker's classic 1979 film, *Midnight Express*.

Based on the true story of William Hayes, the movie is about an American caught smuggling a small amount of hash out of Turkey in the early 70s, and who eventually escapes from the brutal prison in which he'd been incarcerated for five years. While there, his spirit and sanity were tested to their limits. At one point in the film, Hayes finds himself in "the wheel," a congregation of prisoners who are nothing more than a shadow of their former selves, walking listlessly and aimlessly in a huge circle. Desperate not to lose himself entirely, Hayes determines that he cannot be a mindless cog in the giant "wheel" and begins to walk in the opposite direction. As he does,

Ahmet, a fellow prisoner who has now descended into madness, calls out his contrary behavior:

"Where are you going? Why don't you walk the wheel with us? What is the matter my American friend? What has upset you? Oh, a bad machine doesn't know that he's a bad machine. You still don't believe it? You still don't believe you're a bad machine? To know yourself is to know G-d, my friend. The factory knows, that's why they put you here. You'll see. You'll find out. In time, you'll know."

But Billy isn't having any of it. "Oh, I know. I already know. I know that you are a bad machine," he tells Ahmet. "That's why the factory keeps *you* here. And do you know how I know? Huh? I know, because I'm from the factory. I make the machines!" It is at this moment that Billy Hayes realizes he must escape the prison to survive. There's no rule that we should follow unwillingly, mindlessly. Doing so is the absolute betrayal of truth—of the truth within us. Let that sit for a moment.

Meanwhile, let's talk about destiny in terms of what kind of a legacy brand we want to leave behind.

DESTINY'S CHILD

For many years, I wrestled with the notion of destiny, presuming that I had one—a very specific one—and believing that, out of fear, I self-sabotaged and denied my one true path as an actor/screenwriter/comedian. That was bullshit. The truth is, I spent too much of my life striving to become something I really wasn't. I wrote this book, in part, to point out how we negatively affect the kind of legacy brand we will leave behind when we get caught up in trying to catch up to some "destiny" we think we must embrace. I believe the real truth about destiny is not that we spend our lives becoming "a sock salesman" or "a doctor," or "the most awarded copywriter in the breakfast cereal category." Rather, we spend our lives becoming who we really are. We spend our lives becoming *ourselves*. And our true selves often know better than we do what they want to become.

I used to think I was the only person who struggled when trying to convey what I do. I've been a publicist, a standup comedian, a screenwriter, an actor, a copywriter, a strategist podcaster. I assumed my superpower was entertaining people in one form or another. It isn't. My superpower is listening. That's why I finally recognized that who I really am, what I have actually spent my professional life becoming, is a really good listener, who through that superpower, provides MESSAGE Therapy. I listen to people talk about their intentions, and in my head, I hear the "voice" of their personal brand—their legacy brand. Then I help them be true to that brand. That's it. Honest, simple, and valuable. I advocate an approach to business, to the messages you convey within business (and in your personal life) that are truthful, not merely to grab the attention of your target audience, but also to be *worthy* of their attention, whether it's for 30 seconds, 10 minutes, or the lifespan of their soul.

DOLPHIN IN A SHARKSKIN JACKET

If this semoir boils down to one imperative, it's to encourage you to abandon fear and choose reality in your efforts to leave behind a worthy legacy brand. The truth should never be a threat. It is, as I put forth at the start, your weapon of choice as you wage battle in defense of your truest, most authentic personal brand—your legacy brand.

As you move through your adventures in this scary, crazy, beautiful, ridiculous world, remember that each of us must *sell daily*. You must do this to survive and to thrive. You must sell your superpowers and your imperfections with equal vigor.

Coming to terms with truth in your business, in your relationships, in your brands will absolutely, positively make you better at selling your product...and as a matter of course, it will make you a better *you*. It will ensure that the legacy brand you leave behind will be one you can be proud of. And there's no bigger win than that.

I once believed that the world was made of dolphins and sharks. The dolphins were heart-centered and decent; the sharks were "killers," constantly on the move and the make, seizing the riches of the world by any means necessary. I now recognize that, with very few exceptions, each of us is a dolphin. Face it: if you did not want to be the best you, leaving behind the best legacy, you wouldn't have picked up this book. I don't care what you do for a living, what temperament you have, what mistakes you've made or continue to make, or how tough an exterior you have. If you're reading this, you are a dolphin.

But to survive and thrive in this post-truth world, we each must create for ourselves a tough, sharkskin jacket. Reading this book, you're getting down with your dolphin self, but hopefully at the same time you are keeping that sharkskin jacket close by, looking clean and sharp, and, like Billy Joel says at the end of every show, not "taking any shit from anybody."

BETWEEN NOW AND THE NEXT BOOK

Trial and error in life and in business have brought me to this point, and that's what I've tried to share with you. A little common sense has also been applied. All I care about now is that you get from this book what you'd hoped you would when you shelled out the money for it. For my part, I'll be thrilled if you come away in possession of an improved partnership with reality. This read is also a great success if you are leaning into the idea that for you to win, someone else *also* has to win, and that can only come by championing the truth. And it's an immense success if you rise from this reading with an understanding that we are all connected to each other and have more in common and are walking more similar paths than we realize. This is the kind of truth that we should all be selling. With that, I hope you'll be kinder to yourself and feel like you wanna give the world a hug, because with the benefit of the doubt, each of us is worthy of a warm embrace.

Oh, and I also want to encourage you to keep this book. Meaning, if you close it and think, "Dude, this was an awesome book!" and you give it to someone you think will appreciate it… when the next two books in this series come out, you will be left with an incomplete set. You can easily *gift* someone with their own fresh copy, not this dog-eared and possibly scribbled-in, personalized version. And please don't merely put this on your shelf, letting it just sit there! If what I've shared has really had an impact on you, keep it close, like an arrow in your professional quiver, improving not only your business but your personal relationships and increasing the gratification you get from the work you do and the people you care about.

Speaking of impact, we sure do hear a lot about it these days, along with "purpose." I'm hoping that if you've been impacted by this book, that's because you have allowed yourself to consider just how important the truth really is to you, how honest you want to be about who you really are, and whether those you surround yourself with are authentic or just bullshitting you. I hope the book influences the way you will now go forward with your business, relationships, brands (both personal and professional), and, especially, your heart.

If we're gonna talk about our impact and the purpose that helps us make that impact, let's really figure out what that purpose is. I was a guest on the *Conscious Conversion* podcast in 2023, and the host, my friend Sara Yamtich—who is a geyser of earthy energy—asked me, "What's your purpose?" Knowing Sara's soulfulness and her rich background across several fields, I wanted to give her a thoughtful answer. "To lower the temperature," I finally said. It's my instinct to cool things off wherever temperatures (and tempers) flare, wherever egos get exaggerated, or perspectives get perverted. I'd like to think that I've achieved some measure of success in lowering the temperature in my circle of influence by using humor first and then by challenging others to think, question, and develop in a safe space that's filled with warmth. I attempt this with my clients, on my *Truth Tastes Funny* podcast, and on stages all over the world. I'm hoping through this book I can do the same for you, to challenge you, in a safe space filled with warmth, to think more intentionally, question more intently, and dedicate yourself to digging deep, pushing aside your distractions and delusions, so you'll be able to land on the buried treasure, that hard surface beneath the dirt...where lies the truth.

If you can do this, you will be worthy of "selling your offer," whatever it may be.

NOTES

Chapter 2

Online Etymology Dictionary, https://www.etymonline.com/word/brand. *"Old English: brond, fire, flame, destruction by fire; firebrand, piece of burning wood, torch. Proto-Germanic: brandaz, 'a burning.'"*

David Ogilvy, *Ogilvy on Advertising*, (Vintage Books, a division of Random House: New York City, 1983). *"... The intangible sum of a product's attributes—its name, packaging and price, its history, its reputation, and the way it's advertised."*

Erin Johnstone, "Hypnosis for Children," Healing Soul Hypnosis, https://healingsoulhypnosis.com//services/hypnosis-for-children/#:~:text=Children%20in%20utero%20until%20 2,years%2C%20 they%20move%20into%20beta, (2024).

Chapter 3

David Asarnow, "Brand Voice Runway" podcast, October 5, 2023 *"I don't believe in New Year's resolutions. I believe in setting the plan and implementing that plan and adjusting that plan on a daily* *and monthly basis because our minds change and the fact of the matter is most resolutions don't work. If we set a big goal for ourselves and we're halfway through it, and we haven't even scratched the surface, then unconsciously our mind doesn't believe that were going to be able to achieve it. So, we have to chunk it down into smaller, achievable objectives."*

Chapter 8

Lawrence J. Epstein, *The Haunted* Smile, (Public Affairs-Persius Book Group: New York City, 2001). *"The comedians offered audiences consolation through laughter in times of distress... They bound diverse members of the American community to one another; Americans who could laugh together didn't fight. Finally, the comedians gave their audiences a weapon, characteristically satire, to confront life's unfairness."*

ABOUT THE AUTHOR

Known as "The MESSAGE Therapist™," Hersh Rephun is a speaker, author, and consultant who specializes in crafting incomparable personal brands for innovators, disrupters, and thought leaders. He's worked with startups and billion-dollar brands, challengers and market leaders, fledgling filmmakers and Oscar nominees.

Hersh spent a decade as a standup comedian, appearing at The Comedy Store, The Improvisation, Ice House, Comedy Cellar, and The Comic Strip, and playing gigs across the country.

He hosts the popular *Truth Tastes Funny* and *YES, BRAND* podcasts. Hersh operates on one simple principle: sell the truth with humor and humanity.

Hersh is a married father of five and follows the sun.

www.ingramcontent.com/pod-product-compliance
Lightning Source LLC
Chambersburg PA
CBHW071703210326
41597CB00017B/2304